The Reel Revolution

THE
REEL REVOLUTION

A Film Primer on Liberation

Neil P. Hurley

ORBIS BOOKS
Maryknoll, New York 10545

The Catholic Foreign Mission Society of America (Maryknoll) recruits and trains people for overseas missionary service. Through Orbis Books Maryknoll aims to foster the international dialogue which is essential to mission. The books published, however, reflect the opinions of their authors and are not meant to represent the official position of the Society.

Library of Congress Cataloging in Publication Data

Hurley, Neil P
  The reel revolution.

  Includes bibliographical references.
  1. Moving-pictures—Moral and religious aspects.
2. Liberation theology. I. Title.
PN1995.5.H79   791.43'0909'3'   77-17634
ISBN 0-88344-432-1
ISBN 0-88344-433-X pbk.

To the memory of
Padre Hernán Larraín, S.J.,
Chilean priest, publicist, and psychologist,
who defined liberation
in terms of truth and not ideology

An education that is used to domesticate merely transfers knowledge. . . . A conscientizing—and therefore liberating—education is not that transfer of neatly wrapped knowledge in which there certainly is no knowledge; it is a true act of knowing. . . . As I conscientize myself, I realize that my brothers who don't eat, who don't laugh, who don't sing, who don't love, who live oppressed, crushed and despised, who are less each day, are suffering all this because of some reality that is causing it. And at that point I join in the action historically by genuinely loving, by having the courage to commit myself (which is no easy thing!) or I end up with a sense of guilt because I am not doing what I know I should.

—PAULO FREIRE

Contents

Preface

Liberation has become so much a part of the contemporary movie scene that in its October 25 cover story on the 1976 re-make of *King Kong*, *Time* described the destructive binge of the forty-foot ape atop Manhattan's World Trade Center "as a projection of Western fears of what might happen if the Third World should develop its potential power and strike back." The new version of *King Kong* reflects a sensibility absent in the classic 1933 version, which was a romance-adventure tale based on the *Beauty and the Beast* legend. In that film, a movie producer wanted to imprison Kong as a freak in a theatre; in the new Kong, oil company executives see in the great ape a symbol of corporate might and so provoke his spectacular escape. The appeal of Kong has been broadened to make him a political symbol, what the authors of the *Time* cover story called "a not entirely farfetched projection of nations and races that the capitalist countries have for years exploited."

The prisoner thinks obsessively of only one thing —escape: thus the abiding appeal of *King Kong*. This book proposes to show that movies are liberating. True, motion pictures have been seen as "escape"—but only, as a rule, in the most superficial sense of distraction, entertainment, and as a way of "killing time." Granted that movies are often a parenthesis in our grey lives of duty and obligation, they often succeed not only in taking us out of our everyday familiar world but also introduce us into a deeper level of the psychological and spiritual realities that are at work beneath the repetitive, often monotonous, appearances of existence. Whether on the small TV or large theatre screen, movies at their artistic best tap the deepest chords of humanity, sympathy, and understanding, introducing us into the world of the child (Chaplin's *The Kid, 400 Blows, Shoeshine, Forbidden Games*), of the poor *(The Good Earth, The Grapes of Wrath, Dead End, Bicycle Thief, The Pawnbroker)*, of the rich *(The Women, Citizen Kane, Sunset Boulevard, The Damned)*, of hate *(Triumph of the Will, Monsieur Verdoux, The Servant, The Godfather)*, of love *(Seventh Heaven, Camille, Ballad of a Soldier, Hiroshima, Mon Amour)*, of the anguished soul *(M, The Informer, On the Waterfront, Seven Beauties)*, of race *(Raisin in the Sun, West Side Story, The Great White Hope, Sounder)*, and of high sanctity *(The Passion of Joan of Arc, The Diary of a Country Priest, A Man for All Seasons)*.

Such films make out a strong argument for the case that film is the new humanism and that in speaking to literates and illiterates alike it can tease out of us a sense of greater possibilities, alternative selves, and new horizons. My contention, to be demonstrated in the following pages, is that movies as "the reel revolution" meet the requirements of true education—which is to aid in the escape of the best possible self among the many latent personalities in each of us. D. W. Griffith asserted that his purpose as a director was to make his audiences see. By that he meant to see the implicit, the non-manifest, the invisible relationships. Motion pictures imprint on us indelible patterns of feeling, thinking, and judging that become part of our character, not seldom in ways that are opposed to the true liberating ends of a humanistic education. For good or bad, King

Kong, Frankenstein, the Walt Disney stable of cartoon characters, Mary Poppins, the immortal stars (Gable, Garbo, Cagney, Monroe, Bogart, Bardot), and the action stars of westerns, cop films, and karate serials—all have contributed in immeasurable ways to the filmic folklore that millions upon millions of impressionable viewers have imbibed.

While movies have long reached the threshold of recognition as a serious art form, they have not been as yet fully perceived as a "revolution." The reason is that the critics and students of cinema have not looked for liberation techniques and themes in movies. The stress has been on topics such as the sociology of film as a mass medium phenomenon in urban-industrial society, the economics of the industry, the art classics of motion picture history, film nostalgia, biography, and attention to directors (as in the case of the *auteur* theory). I submit that the "reel revolution" rests on three criteria:

1. Beneath the mass "escape" syndrome that makes movie production profitable is a subtle but very real judgment on the larger society that supports film.

2. Beneath the flow of sights and sounds with which movies drench us are enduring themes of conformity, acceptance, frustration, protest, rebellion, and the appetite for justice.

3. Beneath the constraints of movie-makers (writers, stars, producers, and directors) to make money is the irrepressible urge to make enduring statements of universal and profound significance on the human condition.

The "reel revolution" has been with us for many decades but it has essentially gone unperceived outside of elite circles. One of the greatest noncomformists in the history of movies, Robert Flaherty, believed that of all the technologies at humanity's disposal the motion pic-

ture camera afforded the greatest potential for liberation. Flaherty subordinated everything to this conviction and reached the theatre screens of the world despite his unwillingness to imitate the commercial formula of Hollywood. He rejected the "tempero-centrism"
of our age, in which the preliterate was seen as primitive
and ignorant and thus provided modern movie-goers
with critical norms for their own complex existences
through such memorable documentaries as *Nanook of
the North, Moana, Men of Aran, The Land,* and *Louisiana
Story.*

Even in the more commercially-oriented entertainment types of feature films there are deeper themes of
communication, often missed by the larger public and at
times not even intended by the professional technicians,
artists, and talents involved in the multimillion-dollar
enterprise of making films. We wish to point out a
"liberating" way of looking at well-known films so that
the ordinary "escape" motive behind movie-watching is
considered not only as an escape from the routine
schedule of our consumer society but as an escape into a
deeper understanding of the psychological and spiritual
laws that are at work both beneath the images and
behind the sound track of motion pictures. I hope the
reader will use the index to see the films mentioned, for
there is no substitute for this.

I wish to thank Christopher Mooney, S.J., who invited
me to be a visiting professor of pastoral theology at
Woodstock College at the time he was president of that
institution. My three semesters at that Jesuit theolo-
gate enabled me to deepen the intuitions I had regarding film and liberation theology. I am also grateful to
several professors at Florida State University where I
lectured on liberation themes in 1975. Particularly fruit-
ful were my discussions with my colleagues Dr. Richard

Rubenstein and Dr. Lawrence Cunningham. Dr. John Mosier of Loyola University (New Orleans) shared with me his broad knowledge of Brazilian and European cinema. I also thank Helen W. Cyr of the Enoch Pratt Free Library in Baltimore for her invaluable documentary contribution to a cinematic liberation theology by her compilation of *A Filmography of the Third World: An Annotated List of 16 mm. Films* (Metuchen, N.J.: The Scarecrow Press, 1976). Dr. Walter Maestri, Associate Dean of the College of Liberal Arts, also at Loyola University, helped me to finish the final draft. I am also indebted to Philip Scharper, Editor-in-Chief, and John Eagleson, Editor, both of Orbis Books, Maryknoll, New York, for their assistance. Constance Burke and Wesley Sandel helped considerably with their patient preparation of the Index.

Introduction

Liberation is the piston propelling the engine of history. The dawn of civilization appeared when the inhabitants of the riverine valleys of the Nile, Mesopotamia, and the Indus organized themselves to escape the precarious dependence on nature's bounty and primitive agricultural economies. Historical consciousness was born when the Hebrew people were led out from the slavery of Egypt under the leadership of Moses. Christ introduced a doctrine of universal love and basic equality, which infused the Greco-Roman tradition of reason, law, and science. The repeated problems of church-state affiliation up to and through the Middle Ages led to an eventual separation of altar and throne, setting the stage for the Renaissance, the Protestant Reformation, and the Industrial Revolution. The constant revolt against the arbitrary exercise of authority led to the Magna Carta, the English Common Law, the American and French Revolutions.

Since then the theme of liberation has dominated the pages of world history as little else: the nineteenth-century independence movements of Europe and Latin America down through the Mexican and Russian Revolutions, the Irish Sinn Fein movement, the appearance of new states such as India after World War II and the more recent bloody freedom battles in Algeria, Angola, China, Cuba, Ireland, South Africa, Israel, and Vietnam, to mention the more dramatic examples. And

1

within countries, we have the movements of the minority races and the consciousness-raising activities of women, youth, and other protest groups. Without doubt, the issue of liberation will continue to be the focal point of human activity for the remainder of this century. For this reason, it is imperative that we understand it apart from its ideological biases in which "we-they" distinctions becloud the more basic elements of justice and human dignity to which all liberation groups inevitably appeal.

If "liberation" is a highly-charged and ambivalent word, it is due mainly to the fact that its associations come from the unexamined premises of those who employ the word. Karl Mannheim in his classic work, *Ideology and Utopia,* has shown with great perception that "mind-sets" can be broadly divided into those which promote change (utopian movements) and those which resist change (ideological movements). The differences in perception recall the well-known experiment with the partially-filled glass of water: Whereas some tend to see the glass half-empty, others are inclined to see it as half-filled. This happens with radical and reactionary groups. The latter will feel uncomfortable with the word "liberation" and be change-resistant while the former will be exhilarated by it and will be change-prone. In each case, the value of "liberation" in its fullest humanistic sense is highly jaundiced by the subconscious but real interests of each of the "labelling groups," which project onto the world their own, frequently inarticulated, fears or desires. Too few people relativize their position in responsible and open ways to see themselves as others see them. How often do people hear their voices on tape or see their photos and disclaim their own identity. That's not me! Yes, the audiotape and the snapshot reply with peculiar objectivity: That's you—with your warts, wrinkles, and furrowed brow.

What is needed is some trustworthy criterion to enable persons and groups to recognize in their perceptual and judgmental habits the emotional filters that distort liberation discussions. We submit that motion pictures can serve to induce this healthy "shock of recognition" and provide us with examples of principles, techniques, and models of liberation. This represents no small gain toward demystifying the definitions of liberation furnished by either of the two "labelling groups," be they radical or conservative, utopian or reactionary. We propose in this introductory chapter a working model of liberation designed to organize the insights that we shall examine in the following pages from a discussion of key films.

Our approach is somewhat similar to what the great Russian director Sergei M. Eisenstein called "cinedialectics"—the use of images to stimulate thought. Whereas Eisenstein used this method to promote a sympathetic sense of the Bolshevik revolution, our purpose is to illuminate the deep-seated drive for liberation within individuals and groups in different types of socio-political systems, of which socialist societies are but one expression. Film has become an international language, understood by all. The ease and economy with which motion pictures reach illiterates and literates, rich and poor, old and young alike means that we have a unique tool of "consciousness-raising," capable both of universal access and, as we shall see, of depth penetration in terms of education.

An apt film for study is *John Reed: Insurgent*, a Mexican film that shows the growth in political awareness of an American journalist who, while in Mexico to report on Pancho Villa and the revolution, gradually became convinced of the justice of the uprising and dedicated himself to similar causes around the world as an international correspondent. From being a "participant-observer," John Reed grew to take a stand *in* history, not alongside of it. His story is a fascinating study in the psychology of conversion.

Here we shall consider five key elements in understanding liberation as a science and not as an ideology.

—The first step in any liberation process is the adoption of a *critical stance*, an awareness of what must be changed or abandoned. Liberation from what? The answer depends on the threshold of suffering, which is always a relative judgment. A well-known adage has it: "It depends on whose ox is gored." While there are groups with a low threshold for injustice, who have "bruised souls" and bristle at the slightest provocation, there are groups that are docile, resigned, and long-suffering. It is a question of the "sticking point": When do people refuse to be resigned to a situation and begin actively to resist it? In a study of the revolt of a group of miners in Bolivia, it was found that the "sticking point" arose where the choice was between slow death in the mine and dying in a battle of resistance against intolerable conditions. This is seen vividly in the Polish film *Pearls in the Crown* (1974) and in the Bolivian film *Courage of the People* (1971). I once talked with Father John M. Corridan, S.J., the "waterfront priest" who partly inspired the film *On the Waterfront*. He told me that the choice offered the longshoremen on the New York piers was "to go down" or "to go down fighting."

Gillo Pontecorvo's *Kapó* is a shocking study of life in a German concentration camp. It deals with the choices for survival, either through submission or death with honor. A woman trustee, having gained the confidence of the Nazi authorities, risks her life to permit an escape from the camp when she shuts off the electric current in the encircling wire fence. Her own death is the occasion of the freedom of others. The Italian director Lina Wertmuller treated a similar theme in *Seven Beauties* (1976). Here we have a reversal of roles and choices. The Neapolitan romantic, played by Giancarlo Giannini, is obsessed with honor at first, but in a German concentration camp he becomes obsequious, making love to a brutal female Nazi commander and choosing those fellow Italians in his stalag who would be eliminated. The Wertmuller film seems to be a counterstatement to the message in *Kapó* and suggests that not only the "fittest" survive but also those who are most apt at accommodating to the opportunities at hand.[1]

No one is expressly for oppression and yet it exists, in fact it is growing. Why? Injustice has an objective and subjective side. We hope through our study to arrive at some conclusions regarding such questions as who, how, and when regarding the "sticking point" in a decision of liberation. One thing is certain: Without awareness, there is no liberation. *Nulla ignoranti cupido!* Ignorance has never stirred desire. We remind the reader of our maxim: "The prisoner thinks obsessively of only one thing—escape!"

—The second element in any liberation process is a lucid version of the *goal of liberation*. A stunning example is found in Eisenstein's *Strike* (1924), especially in the scene where the worker raises his hand as the symbol that power lies with the people if only they will cease being passive. Equally dramatic as an example is Sergei Eisenstein's *October* (1927), a film that follows the events described in John Reed's *Forty Days That Shook the World* and often is called by that title. This movie shows government troops in readiness to repel the attacking Bolshevist revolutionaries. The Kerensky government had succeeded the rule of the Tsar but was too weak to effect far-reaching social changes. Eisenstein's *October* is a splendid example of the "sticking point," dramatically emphasized by the scenes of women soldiers mounting the barricades. Enthusiasm spreads from the first resisters to others who are eager for rapid change. The palace in *October* was a visible symbol of the oppressive status quo and focused the discontent of the Bolshevik rebels.

Many movements fail to obtain the redress of their legitimate grievances because of a blurred focus of the "liberation outcome," which was emotionally but not intellectually perceived. Often frustration, anger, and resentment have powered movements of protest and revolution without proposing alternatives that might appeal to those like-minded advocates of change who, while condemning the *status quo ante*, are reluctant to lend their support to "search and destroy" actions that presume that out of the ashes of destruction must necessarily come something better. It is known that Russia has proposed noncapitalistic forms of social change in "Third World" countries as the entering wedge toward traditional Marxist-controlled society. Similarly, the United States has urged democratic measures with the idea of identifying capitalism and even consumerism with the political concept of an open society. The world is looking for a new model. Some efforts have been made in Czechoslovakia under Dubcek, in Chile under Allende, in Tanzania under Nyerere, and in Italy with its inevitable *compromesso storico* among Christian Democrats, Communists, and Socialists.

—As important as strategy is, the question of *tactics* arises. There is no privileged single road to liberation, although at times revolutionary exponents of liberation can give that impression. The films to be discussed will enable us to see the pluralism of means that are at hand. For one person it is rhetoric; for another it is confrontations such as a strike; for a third it is nonviolent suffering in the tradition of Gandhi, Martin Luther King, or Cesar Chavez; for others it is violence, as in the case of Fidel Castro, Che Guevara, or Camilo Torres. The means toward a proposed end can never be indifferent. The "how" can change the "what," though often this happens imperceptibly as a sort of long-term "sleeper effect." For instance religion can be a means of reinforcing oppressive systems of injustice, as we see in Miklos Jancsó's *Agnus Dei*, where an allegorically fanatical priest alternates between passionate ascetical feats coupled with devotional demonstrations and blessing prisoners before being executed. In all Jancsó's films there are decisive "breaks" with the past; the situation is resolved one way or the other, as in *The Red and the White* (1968), *Silence and the Cry* (1969), *Winter Wind* (1970), and *Red Psalm* (1971).[2]

In the United States, however, films are more intrapsychic and only rarely deal with larger social issues, as in *Bound for Glory* and *Harlan County, USA*, both released in 1976. The problems of the working class and labor unions are underrepresented in American cinema. *The Molly Maguires* (1970), directed by Martin Ritt, concentrates more on the character of the spy from the Pinkerton Detective Agency (Sean Connery) than the cause of a group of determined Irish coal miners who used violence to change the wretched conditions in the Pennsylvania anthracite region of the 1870s. In this country the national trusts (railroads, oil, sugar, and steel) reached the peak of their capitalist growth before unions were recognized. This was not true of Latin American nations such as Argentina, Brazil, and Chile, where workers' rights came to be recognized before the industrialization process reached maturity. Only by persistent dedication to an ideal of justice do U.S. minority movements grow to the point where they can exercise countervailing power and neutralize the exercise of arbitrary authority. The problem of the migratory workers and fruitpickers, poignantly depicted in *The Grapes of Wrath* (1940), is an apt example of the long-term process of righting human wrongs in America. The boycott of grapes, lettuce, and wine, the inspired leadership of Cesar Chavez, and the sympathy efforts of many were effective tactics in the cause of the migratory workers.

Tactics often depend upon the strategic environment in which the group intent on liberation finds itself. In the United States, minorities generally resort to tactical expediency. For example, the blacks in the United States can choose courses of action closed to resident Orientals (e.g., appealing to Congresspersons of their racial origin). In this regard, the time-frame is decisive in what means are to be adopted. Slaves, as in the film *Spartacus* (1960), are more desperate than the dock workers in *On the Waterfront* (1954), the miners in *Salt of the Earth* (1957), or the factory workers in *The Organizer* (1970). A study of these films can sensitize the viewer to the role of violence in social change. Pacific programs to redress grievances can escalate into scenarios of force, murder, and civil disorder.

—Liberation movements cannot be adequately understood without a consideration of their *leaders*. The inarticulated angers and frustrations of a group, a class, a race, an ideology, or a nation must be given expression in the form of some person. Andrezej Wajda's films on the Polish underground in World War II are stunning cinematic studies of how human nature resists oppression. *Canal* and *Ashes and Diamonds* show that a people prefer to suffer and die rather than live in indignity. There are at times situations in life in which death by resistance is the sole path to maintaining authentic identity.[3]

The same lessons are seen throughout history: the Roman slave Spartacus or an Arab religious leader, the Mahdi; a saintly woman such as Joan of Arc or a nonconformist such as Luther; a charismatic leader such as T. E. Lawrence or revolutionaries such as Che Guevara or Fidel Castro or a civil rights leader such as Martin Luther King, Jr. Motion pictures have treated all these types of liberationists. In each case the respective leader showed the single-mindedness and exceptional strength of will to attract followers, many of whom were prepared to risk their possessions and lives for the cause.

The memory of a selfless leader may live on even long after the death of that person. Two excellent examples are Guiliano Montaldo's *Sacco and Vanzetti* (1972) and Bo Widerberg's *Joe Hill* (1972). The Italian immigrants and anarchists Sacco and Vanzetti and the Wobbly organizer Joe Hill, a Swedish immigrant, were framed for murders they did not commit and thus became social martyrs whose romanticized legends inspired subsequent generations bent on resistance to the oppressive collusion of the press, the law, public opinion, and the state. Lincoln and Gandhi are two examples of martyrs for the cause of social justice whose names are enshrined in history. Contemporary United States and India would not be recognizable today without the incalculable influence each exercised over the history of their native lands during critical moments in which self-determination was the issue. The inspirational liberation leader can crystallize hope in situations that otherwise would seem without remedy.

—An often neglected and crucial theme in any complete model of liberation is the *full spectrum of effects.* As in most human affairs, struggles for freedom, justice, and equality produce both deliberate and unintended effects. The Chinese have a saying that if we knew beforehand the range of effects of our actions, we would not act. Human decisions are usually the product of incomplete information and thus lead necessarily to certain blind consequences. While I was in Chile during the Marxist-dominated regime of Salvador Allende, Fidel Castro was a visitor in 1972. At a public meeting, he was asked about the people who were executed under his command. He said that no ruler likes to kill, not even President Batista whom he had overthrown as an enemy of the people. Castro was admitting that there are unintended, even unwished, consequences of any liberation project. In the Franco-Bulgarian co-production, *It's Raining Over Santiago* (1975), the military coup by General Pinochet in September 1973 showed the effects of Allende's surprise election three years earlier. Just as Castro did not want to imprison, exile, or kill members of the opposition, so too Pinochet's junta was constrained by circumstances to adopt policies which violated human rights.

There is a saying about revolution: "Anyone who wants to bake a cake must break eggs." The same is true of right-wing coups. Those who play the role of the revolutionary or reactionary breakers often underestimate the number of eggs. All too often what poses as liberation is nothing more than pseudo-liberation in which one form of injustice is substituted by another —different but essentially opposed to the full humanization of the people. This is powerfully illustrated in *Mexico, the Frozen Revolution* (1970). The documentary shows sepia-colored footage of Pancho Villa's uprising and continues Mexico's history down to the one-party domination of Mexico's political system in the modern period. It complements *John Reed: Insurgent.*

Revolution implies victims. One is a corollary of the other. The victims may be bloody ones, such as in the French Revolution when the members of the ruling class were guillotined (as in the 1937 film *Marie Antoinette*). Or the victims may be those whose property and possessions are expropriated, as has happened so often with minority groups in the case of the more benign forms of persecution such as discrimination (e.g., Stanley Kramer's *Pressure Point*—1962). Seldom in history do we find the disinterested revolutionary models in which "auto-victimhood" is proposed. Alexander Dovzhenko's classic silent film, *Earth*, shows the selfless sacrifice of Russian farmers after the Revolution. There are numerous cinematic examples of selfless protest which include portrayals of Christ, Thomas More, Billy Budd, St. Vincent de Paul, Albert Schweitzer, and Abbé Pierre. A remarkable instance of charisma is found in *The Autobiography of Jane Pittman*, about a 113-year-old former slave who drinks from a water fountain reserved for whites in a Southern community. As she walks away, supported by her cane, one senses that she has earned her right to perform this symbolically charged act of civil defiance in memory of all those who died and suffered unjustly as victims of racial injustice.

These, then, are the five key elements in understanding liberation as a science and not as an ideology: (1) the diagnosis of the evil; (2) the strategic goal to remedy the malady; (3) the tactical means to achieve the liberation purpose; (4) the leader endowed with the ability to execute the strategic and tactical plan; and (5) the full range of consequences, intended and unintended. The word "liberation," we repeat, is a relative concept. People interpret it according to some "we-they" stance. If *they* exercise power, then liberation is salutary. If, however, *we* control and use it, then it is oppressive. The word "liberation" has become suspect, especially in conservative circles, because of the radical, often utopian, ideological contraband that has been smuggled into the word. The "we-they" situation ensues and with it an adversary situation with the usual symptoms of passionate responses, mutual misperception, and inevitable escalation of fear, distrust, and not infrequently violence. Here motion pictures can help us to understand more objectively the pattern of "stimulus-and-response" in "we-they" adversary situations in which both parties assume righteousness and a hallowed cause. All violence wears the mask of legitimacy and rationalization.

Liberation is a serious theme and deserves more sober and sustained study than it has commanded in the past. It is, without any doubt, an imperative of history and is inscribed in the very nature of the human condition. The problem is how to transcend the self-serving definitions of liberation that not only threaten those in the ascendancy but have very precarious foundations in terms of logic, justice, and morality. William Blake, the famous writer and mystic, once commented: "The same law for the ox and the lion is oppression." As a result, the boundaries of freedom and opportunity are difficult to set. One person's liberation is another's repression. Some of the great conquerors of history saw themselves as liberators—Alexander the Great, Julius Caesar, Tamerlane, Genghis Khan, Attila the Hun, and Napoleon. The de-Stalinization process brought to light the human costs of consolidating the Russian Revolution. Pontecorvo's *The Confession* (1971) showed how people were "criminalized" and tortured by bureaucratic whim. Yves Montand's role as an innocent victim in a Russian satellite country was based on fact. The chronicles of history would seem to indicate that more grievances are created and perpetuated in the name of liberation than are actually redressed. In a world of galloping strides in the progress of science and technology, it is time to develop a worldwide consensus on the science of liberation.

As a primer toward the creation of such a science, motion pictures enjoy certain advantages. They are becoming a universal experience as TV becomes more accessible to the illiterates, to the poor and the disenfranchised of the earth. These are the people who most need to learn the art of self-organization in order to combat the institutional and structural ills that bear on them the heaviest. Within the culture of poverty, movies and TV play an extraordinary role—one which has been underresearched. By the twist of a dial people can see movies on the small screen in the comfort of their homes and without paying admission. India is the largest producer of movies in the world. Moreover, in India as of 1976, the government, with the aid of a U.S. experimental satellite, relayed TV broadcasts to 2,400 remote villages. This adds greater weight to the observation of the filmmaker Robert Flaherty regarding the unique capability of the movie camera to humanize people in an increasingly urban-technological world.[4]

There exists a vast audiovisual patrimony worth billions of dollars in celluloid motion pictures, which, though made for commercial and entertainment purposes, nevertheless contains insights and lessons eminently suited to awaken us from our "sleep-walking" state as baffled citizens who are in a quandary about the structural forces that enmesh and control us. Like the idea of liberation, the word "entertainment" itself is a multi-valued word. What entertains one person can educate—even liberate—another. This is true of the durable classics such as *M*, *The Informer*, and *Modern Times*. And who can forget Welles's role as the newspaper tycoon in *Citizen Kane*, and how power corrupts not only the ruthless but those around them. For numerous people, motion pictures can teach and effectively shape character and mental sets, even while they entertain. This is the basic premise of this book.

In the following pages we have selected films that are rather well known and, in most cases, can be seen in neighborhood revivals, at repertory houses, or on TV. Reverting to the origins of motion picture, we treat two classics, *Birth of a Nation* (1915) and *Potemkin* (1925). The latter is by the Russian director, Sergei Eisenstein, and exalts the spirit of the Bolshevik Revolution (coterminous, incidentally, with the rise of movies as a global medium); the former is a product of American genius in the person of D. W. Griffith. Our purpose is to show that, independently of a socialist or a capitalist context, movies at their artistic best are genuine humanistic achievements. While the camera is neutral, its use is not. Film language tends to be ideological, although the mass movie-going audience is not aware of this. Notwithstanding this fact, the critical viewer can become more conscious of this and so make a systematic effort to sift out the chaff of bias from the grain of truth. *Birth of a Nation* and *Potemkin* are silent masterpieces not only of cinematic art but of the science of liberation as well, as we aim to show.

The other films have been chosen to stimulate reflection in terms of the five-part model of liberation described earlier in this chapter. The first step toward any true liberation is an awareness of injustice. "The prisoner thinks obsessively of only one thing—escape!" Not every path of escape can be judged liberating, if in the course of the process it encroaches on others. The films to be discussed will offer dramatic case studies that will enable the reader to grasp the elementary principles of a humanistic liberation. Underlying the criteria implicit in our model are the truths of the Judeo-Christian tradition with its accent on the Exodus event as Moses led the Israelites out of the Egyptian bondage, and on the preaching and deeds of Jesus of Nazareth, who taught universal love, forgiveness, and total liberation—at the secular and spiritual levels as well as the private and social levels.

At the heart of the liberation process is mind and imagination. *The Reel Revolution* seeks to engage both because the challenge of creating alternatives (or "new spaces" as young people like to call the liberation options) is a work of understanding where we are (a mental diagnosis) and conjuring up new possibilities (an act of the imagination). Motion pictures are the product of the human brain and human images.[5] For that reason we firmly believe that movies can help to free us from "mind-binding" assumptions of an ideological nature to answer the grand liberation questions: Liberation —from what?—to what?—how?—under whom?—and with what intended and unintended consequences?

NOTES

1. Cf. Terrence Des Pres, *The Survivor: An Anatomy of Life in the Death Camps* (New York: Oxford University Press, 1976).

2. Cf. Alistair Whyte, *New Cinema in Eastern Europe* (New York: Studio Vista, Dutton Paperback, 1971), pp. 66ff.

3. Ibid., pp. 12ff. Also see Michael J. Stoil, *Cinema Beyond the Danube: The Camera and Politics* (Metuchen, N.J.: The Scarecrow Press, 1974), pp. 134–38.

4. Neil Hurley, *Toward a Film Humanism* (New York: Delta Paperback, 1975).

5. M. Wolfstein and N. Leites, *Movies: A Psychological Study* (New York: The Free Press, 1962).

1.

Peaceful Liberation

A Christian liberation theology recognizes not only the weakness in the oppressor but also the strength in the oppressed. Paulo Freire has pointed out how, in the struggle for humanization, the oppressed must not become in turn oppressors of their oppressors. Often the oppressor's psychology is imprinted in the oppressed in many subtle subconscious ways, as O. Mannoni has brilliantly shown in his study *Prospero and Caliban*. This internalization of what Hegel called the "master-slave" relationship leads to a paralysis of action, a "fear of freedom." We will show how "conscientization" is necessary to break the fetters of fear and to make one aware of the total socio-political context that impedes full humanization of both the master and the slave. The dilemma that presents itself is how can one become liberated without in turn changing into the same type of oppressor that one previously condemned.

There are those who deny that peaceful conflict is effective. When I resided in Chile, many sympathizers of Salvador Allende's Popular Unity government felt that violent takeover was the only effective solution. Since the right-wing military coup, these people believe their opinion has been validated, that change must take place through force. While admitting that peaceful conflict resolution is a difficult and infrequent achievement, we nevertheless believe that it is possible. We have chosen three films to help us appreciate the narrow but open path that employs a type of confrontation appealing to the humanity and liberty of the oppressor as a means to liberating both the master and the slave. We must not give up on nonviolent protest and strategies that appeal to the potential of humanity in each oppressor.

We must be on guard against thinking that resistance is a privileged domain of left-wing radicals. Not everything that dies is useless, nor is everything that is born of value by the fact that it is new. A keen discernment is required. One of the most conservative directors in cinema history is Yasujiro Ozu, known only in Japan until his films were acclaimed in the West after his death in 1963.[1] Representing the belief that we humans must adapt to life's necessities and lessons, Ozu made slow films that revealed a Buddhist wisdom of resignation. His traditional views subordinate the person to the general welfare and thus irritate the modern sensibility. What is often missed about Ozu's films is the belief in a transcendent order of reality in which everything has a place and where mysterious forces of retribution are at work to right the imbalance caused by blind human choices. Though defending past values and critical of change, Ozu's films are important for spiritual liberation.

Ozu's world is that of the patriarchal nuclear family, the same we meet in the novels of Jane Austen and Charles Dickens. He laments the rapid modernization of Japan, the contract-type society that challenges the psychological and spiritual coordinates Ozu respects, ones found in a society where ascriptive rather than acquired status prevails. John Ford has been compared with Ozu, and not without solid reason, for both feel that there are laws that you do not break; rather, if they are violated, they break you. This premise makes for a cyclical view of life, the stoic conviction that if you live long enough, you will see it all—the grievous wheel of existence has only so many spokes.

In *Late Spring* (1949) Ozu shows a widower who out of love for his caring daughter insists that she break her ties with him to get married and raise a family of her own. The last frame shows the father calmly and methodically peeling an apple; the spiralling peels and the circular motions of the knife signify the constant renewal of life. John Ford furnishes a similar sense of stability and natural harmony in such Westerns as *Fort Apache* (1948), *She Wore a Yellow Ribbon* (1949), *Wagonmaster* (1950), and *Rio Grande* (1950). Ford celebrated camaraderie, loyalty, duty, and tribal bonds, although his disenchantment with urban-industrial America was revealed in his post-Western movies: *The Searchers* (1956), *The Man Who Shot Liberty Valance* (1959), and *Cheyenne Autumn* (1964). Just as Ford revealed his basic distaste for new trends, so too did Ozu, who in *The End of Summer* (1961) shows silent black crows in the last scene: The father is dead, the family is dead and, Ozu is saying (two years before his own death), "the old Japan is dead."[2]

In Ozu we have peaceful resistance, a series of melancholic cinematic dirges about the passing of honor and obligation, pride and loyalty of family life, friendship and patriotism. Underneath the film texture is the Oriental "sympathetic sadness," the connectedness of all life, the Buddhist secret that causes monks to burn themselves alive in protest over American and South Vietnamese actions in the Vietnam war. There are subtle expressions of liberation; not all are activist in nature. There are passive forms that operate, as in the case of Ozu and Ford, at the level of artistic insight.³ The revolution is in seeing, as D. W. Griffith knew as he quoted Joseph Conrad's ambition: "I want to make you see."

Another indirect form of liberation is the rebel hero, first embodied in the Hollywood sound film as the likeable gangster-hero, Paul Muni, Edward G. Robinson, James Cagney. These rebels were opposed to society and its unequal legal paths of ascent to fame and fortune. By contrast, John Garfield made no attempt to change society or to hit back.⁴ He suffered inwardly, nurturing his pride, individuality, and private ideals as best he could—usually with the help of some woman attracted to his uncommunicative but virile type of fated sensitivity. Garfield was different than, say, Bogart, Brando, or James Dean. He suffered visibly, not indifferently. Perhaps his Jewish lineage helped to contribute to his unique role as a lover, a nonconformist, but not a revolutionary. Garfield knew something and the audience admired this quiet decision not to get along by going along. Most revolutionaries and liberationists overlook the value of inward suffering and prefer coercion or the struggle to secure power.

This brings us, logically, to a discussion of Sidney Lumet's powerful film, *The Pawnbroker* (1965). Based on a novel by Edgar Lewis Wallant, the film stars Rod Steiger as the owner of a pawnshop in Spanish Harlem. The ghetto is a form of domination through the control of space, by which "one can be compelled to perform a series of actions that are means to the realization of another's plan merely because the other can exclude him from certain space or confine him to a narrow space at will."⁵ The slum is as confining as the mental asylum, the penitentiary, or, as *The Pawnbroker* impresses on the viewer, the concentration camp. Sol Nazerman, the pawnbroker, is badly traumatized by his experiences in a German concentration camp where his wife was degraded and killed. His total recall of the persecution suffered by him, his family, and fellow Jews is curiously intertwined with analogous thoughts about Spanish Harlem as a giant urban concentration camp: the crowded tenements, the tomb-like subways, the littered streets, the abandoned lots, the lives of blacks and browns scarred by drugs, alcohol, prostitution, gambling, and idleness. Unable to shake the somber memories of places such as Dachau, Auschwitz, and Belsen, Sol Nazerman constructs his "anti-project," refusing to become an accomplice in the calloused indifference to the plight of the slum-dwellers. (He himself lives in a quiet residential neighborhood.)

Rod Steiger's performance as the chronically depressed pawnbroker is a *tour de force* of acting. When the black prostitute comes in to his shop and bares her breasts in order to sell herself, the loom of Nazerman's memory shuttles back to the sexual degradation experienced by his late wife at the hands of the Nazi jailors. He wages a one-man crusade against the impersonal but equally totalitarian forces in New York City. At the end of the film, some hold-up men enter the store and threaten the fearless pawnbroker. A Puerto Rican, Jesús Ortíz, intercepts a bullet intended for Nazerman and dies. This gesture of human solidarity shows the potential for liberation even in the blighted culture of the ghetto. Nazerman is intent on keeping his dignity and is touched to see that self-sacrifice and altruism cannot be stifled merely by the greyness of the environment.

The Pawnbroker is a solid contribution to suggesting one concrete approach toward challenging the coercion through space that typifies those American cities that have been aptly described as "black, brown, and broke." Our democratic, free-market arrangements cloak the real coercion that exists. *The Pawnbroker* is a poignant study in quiet dissent. Sol Nazerman is a conscientious objector, one bent on his own personal liberation from the social fictions that shape ghettoes such as Harlem: rent per square foot, occupancy limits per building, and racial barriers that perdure long after the court decisions that bar segregation. *The Pawnbroker* deals with trauma, with "humanistic reserves beneath zombie facades," even though there are no changes in social structures.

Francis Ford Coppola's *The Conversation* also deals with conscience and ironic parallels.[6] Gene Hackman is an expert in electronic surveillance, hired to bug a man and a woman walking in a crowded park. His concern is moral but soon he himself becomes the object of a bugging contract. He futilely strips his apartment to find the recording device. The film ends in a Kafkaesque mood with the professional eavesdropper sitting in the middle of his denuded apartment playing the saxophone, the only human symbol in the entire film. Like Antonioni's *Blow-Up*, Coppola's *The Conversation* shows how technology—either the camera's eye or the tape-recorder's ear—can control space and monitor human behavior in unprecedented ways.

A more direct example of coercion through control of space is seen in prison films. We choose Stuart Rosenberg's *Cool Hand Luke* (1967), because it, like *The Pawnbroker*, illustrates peaceful but effective resistance to an oppressive situation. Paul Newman plays Luke, who is sentenced to a Southern road-gang for having sheared off the tops of parking meters while drunk. The punishment is so far in excess of the crime that the audience immediately identifies with Luke, whose casual charm endears him to us. The prisoners in the camp soon see in Luke a counter-authority symbol. In his well-known book, *Asylums*, Erving Goffman points out how in all such total institutions there is the formal authority structure and the informal structure created by the inmates themselves. This could be considered the instinctive "anti-project," which the liberation impulse creates to shield dignity and autonomy. Luke represents in his unflappable character such a symbol of liberation. A sign of his leadership qualities emerges when he urges the men on the road-gang to work faster to tar the road. The enthusiasm with which they do the work baffles the guards who feel the defiance in this act of spontaneity.

The inevitable confrontation takes place as the camp warden realizes how important it is to humiliate Cool Hand Luke in the eyes of the other prisoners. He knocks Luke down with a cruel blow of his club and then, in a quiet tone, addresses the audience of prisoners, saying: "There seems to be a lack of communication here!" Luke realizes that he is a marked man, but he does not realize that he is just as much a prisoner of the false liberation expectations of the men who adulate him as he is of the barbed wire and armed sentinels. He engineers an escape. The authorities pursue him with attack dogs who follow his scent to a deserted rural church. Luke talks to God there. A guard shoots him in the throat. Luke is deliberately taken to the prison clinic rather than a nearby hospital. In effect, he is murdered by neglect.

The prisoners have mythologized Luke, for, as the still shows, they are smiling and recounting stories of his prowess and feats of "one-up-manship." Whereas Luke was the prisoners' interface with the reality of the prison, they themselves take refuge in dreams, memories, and distractive pastimes. The oppressor is clearly imprinted in them, for they do not aspire to any true liberation. They indulge in escapist hero-worship. It is

instructive to compare *Cool Hand Luke* with other films
such as *I Was a Fugitive from a Chain Gang, From Here
to Eternity, Caine Mutiny, Riot, Birdman of Alcatraz,
Bridge over the River Kwai, King Rat, The Longest Yard*,
and *One Flew Over the Cuckoo's Nest*.

In all these films we see parallel societies within
the larger coercive one. Earlier we spoke of Lina
Wertmuller's *Seven Beauties*. As in the other prison
films mentioned, her brilliant movie sums up the three
responses to systematic brutality: The anarchist
plunges into the cesspool and is machine-gunned to
death; the Italian prisoner protests and begs Pasqualino ("Seven Beauties" himself) to shoot him when
the Nazi officer places the gun in his hand; in the final
scene Pasqualino boasts that he lives, but we wonder,
for something human died in him on the way to survival.
The alternatives are narrow in films about total in-
stitutionalization but inner liberation is never totally
beyond reach, for it can be found in death as *Cool Hand
Luke* proved.

Short of the type of revolt we discussed in Eisenstein's
Potemkin, the only liberation can be some type of
"anti-project" in which the inmates transcend the limits
of their physical confinement. Paul Newman's role as
Cool Hand Luke and Giancarlo Giannini's performance
in *Seven Beauties* offer diametrically opposed paths in
situations where honor and survival clash. Regarding
larger efforts at social liberation and movements geared
to correcting long-standing social injustices, we shall
later study three relevant Third World films: *Earth,
Burn!* and *The Battle of Algiers*.

We have considered different types of domination
through control of space—the ghetto *(The Pawnbroker)*,
the prison *(Cool Hand Luke)*, and the concentration
camp *(Seven Beauties)*. Moreover we alluded to tech-

J. S. Casshyap as Gandhi in Mark Robson's Nine Hours to Rama

nological control in *The Conversation* and *Blow-Up*.
There is another control of space, namely, the domination of less powerful by more powerful countries. Until
World War II such colonialism was a marked characteristic of many of the European nations. Perhaps the
most remarkable empire was that which the British
built (see such films as *Clive of India*, *Khartoum*, and
Zulu). Without a doubt the most dramatic example of
peaceful confrontation in breaking the colonial hold of
any nation was the movement of creative moral protest
lead by Mahatma Gandhi in India. Mark Robson's film,
Nine Hours to Rama (1963), is a fictional recreation of
the assassination of Gandhi by a fanatic opponent,
played by the German actor Horst Buchholz. The film is
a standard Hollywood entertainment movie, but it has a
remarkable feature in the person of an Indian non-
professional actor, J. S. Casshyap, who captures the ascetical radiance of the renowned political and spiritual
leader. The photo on page 25 is of J. S. Casshyap.
Centuries from now, people will find it hard to believe
that a man such as Gandhi really lived, for Machiavel-
lianism and political pragmatism with their belief in the
survival of the fittest have been the predominant political philosophies in world politics thus far in this century.
Idealism in politics is considered atypical, indeed even
an aberration.

Nine Hours to Rama alludes to the main trait of Gan-
dhian protest, namely, the development of a construc-
tive pattern of social relations existing in a high stage of
tension. The tension was produced by the religious conviction of Gandhi that suffering must be spiritually
creative within the personality of the protestor and
without hate for the oppressor. The name given to this
unusual strategy was *satyagraha*, and the tactic was
voluntary suffering as a means of arriving at the truth

and turning weakness into strength. In *An Autobiography: The Story of My Experiments with Truth*, Gandhi tells how he began his discovery of the crucial paradox of spiritual suffering as creative and liberating for both the oppressor and the oppressed. Gandhi, trained in England as a lawyer, led a successful passive resistance movement in South Africa. At that time, though married, he began to live as a celibate, to fast, and in general to cut away the superfluities of life. In India Gandhi encouraged *hartals*, or work-stoppages, to mobilize public opinion and to resist the British. By 1930 Gandhi was a force to be reckoned with, having led thousands of nonviolent protestors in the famous Salt March.

Nine Hours to Rama introduces us to an older Gandhi, one who is beginning to assess the immense difficulties in universalizing a political attitude of nonaggression through purely spiritual means. The basis of Gandhi's search for truth is *ahimsa*, that is "noninjury" to anyone, even the oppressor. *Ahimsa* is both a means and an end. At one and the same time it is transcendent—as an ideal—and immanent—as a tactical force through noncooperation. Mark Robson's film does have a touching moment that captures the spirit of Gandhi's belief that love of the oppressor releases energy in him too. When the assassin, a Hindu, shot Gandhi on his way to his daily prayer meeting, the film represents Gandhi looking compassionately at the fanatical murderer. A man who had looked death in the face with his fast-to-death tactics, instrumental in bringing about the Government of India Act of 1935, could not be at a loss to find the strength to forgive. This single scene justifies our including *Nine Hours to Rama* as a significant film contribution toward understanding one exercise of love, admittedly rare, within the liberation process. Louis Malle's six-hour film, *Phantom India*, lets us see not one but many Indias torn between the weight of preindustrial traditions and western concepts of progress. One Italian hippie in Malle's documentary says he came looking for Gandhi but his ideas were gone. But Gandhi's spirit is not materialized or localized in India; it permeates the evolving consciousness of the species.

The films we have treated have had a common denominator, namely, a reaction to coercion as expressed in a socio-political control of space. *The Pawnbroker* focused on community space. Theoretically the slumdweller is free to move but the problem is that, in the aggregate, slums are part of industrial society, even the most affluent. Sol Nazerman was aware that the racial ghetto has no more reason for existing than the Nazi concentration camp. You can kill a person as effectively in a subhuman environment as in a gas chamber; the only difference is that the former takes longer and is less abhorrent to public opinion. What are the means open to change-agents who want to avoid the Scylla of violence (ghetto riots) and the Charybdis of incremental legal remedies (social welfare programs)? The answer given by Sol Nazerman is one that is unpopular in many circles, namely, absorb the pain and refuse to go along. The contemporary proposal is to fight violence with violence and to discountenance any solution that suggests "auto-victimhood" or martyrdom, whether physical or psychic.

If *The Pawnbroker* offered us a psychodrama of one person's response to human inhumanity, *Cool Hand Luke* gives us a brilliant exposition of a twofold exploitation within the confines of a truly totalized institution (the slum is such only by analogy). Not only is the ingenuous Luke physically restricted, but he allows himself to become the object of his peer-group's fantasies. The friendship—better, the discipleship—is not only superficial and ill-founded but contains the seeds of the tragic death of Luke. Similarly, Pasqualino in *Seven Beauties* is caught between the upper stone of prison authority and the nether stone of comradeship. It is enlightening to compare this dilemma with a similar one in *The Last Detail* (1975), in which two Special Police are responsible for taking an eighteen-year-old sailor to the Marine brig at Portsmouth, Rhode Island. Well-intentioned but naive, the two navy men bring out the prisoner's sense of independence, preparing him for eventual confrontation with the authorities in prison. As a docile person, he would have relatively little trouble in serving his sentence but as a person with a developed self and an independent spirit, the young sailor very likely will run into the problems that beset Paul Newman's Cool Hand Luke.

One of the ways to cultivate a "self" that is "free-in-structures" is religion. True, Karl Marx pointed out the danger of false consciousness in institutional religions that take their values and priorities from the dominant society and its productive system. In calling religion an "opium of the people" (notice that he did not call it an opium *for* the people), Marx knew that religion should not only console; it should also denounce, as did the Old Testament prophets. Faith can help one to choose alternate paths, to construct an "anti-project" that issues in what Freire has called the "humanization of the world." Polish director Jerzy Kawalerowicz directed the spectacle *Pharaoh* (1966) to show the struggle between an enlightened Egyptian ruler and the entrenched priestly class opposed to social reform. Religion is meant to be socially relevant. Was not Christ's death caused by political decisions? Often, however, in its concrete cultural adaptation, Christianity can lead to social mystification and reinforcement of the status quo, just as in the case of the proud priests in *The Pharaoh*.

Nine Hours to Rama shows that contemplation and

deep spirituality need not be "world-shy." Gandhi exercised power and changed the course of India's history,
but not in traditional ways. He did not content himself
with the sublimation of Sol Nazerman nor with the stoi-
cism of Cool Hand Luke, but rather chose to exercise
initiating, not mere countervailing, power. Gandhi saw
that beneath the economic, political, and cultural issues
of imperialism there were serious spiritual laws that
bound the oppressor as well as the oppressed. He tried to
make the dominant power structure feel the reality of
this intangible order and the energy it could produce.
Gandhi once told the foreign correspondent Vincent
Sheean that he had a premonition of his untimely death.
In fact he did not want his life prolonged by medical
science, observing that it may be "that it is better for me
to die." His thought behind this remark was that the
antagonism between the Hindus and the Pakistanis
might cease. His death, so movingly recreated in *Nine
Hours to Rama*, did bring together partisan interests
and strengthened Nehru in his program of unifying a
strife-torn India.

We should not omit reference to a disciple of Gandhi:
Martin Luther King, Jr., whose assassination also ele-
vated the consciousness of humankind to a higher
plateau of vision and transracial unity. There is a remarkable documentary about the career of Martin
Luther King, Jr., as a pacifist "utopian agent." *King* is
the film that spells out the march of his dream from
Montgomery, Alabama, to Memphis, Tennessee. King
admitted his indebtedness to the ideas and example of
Mahatma Gandhi. After he was arrested during the
Montgomery bus boycott, King said: "We must use the
weapon of love. We must have compassion and understanding for those who hate us." The film documentary
King is replete with such statements, reminiscent of

Gandhi's philosophy of *ahimsa,* or noninjury. In the chapter on liberation leadership we shall return to the notion of charisma. King also shared with Gandhi the spiritual conviction that faith emboldens the self to say "I'm not going to give in." King described his philosophy this way: "There is an element of God in every man. No matter how low one sinks into racial bigotry, he can be redeemed." This belief was infectious, for it united the hunger for God with an appetite for fraternity and equality.

We have mentioned a number of films and have concentrated our attention on three in particular. All three have religious overtones. *The Pawnbroker* has as its protagonist a faith-filled Jew; *Cool Hand Luke* shows us a Christ-figure who dies in a countryside chapel and whose memory is cherished by his disciples; *Nine Hours to Rama* brought us into the world of Hindu faith and Gandhi's principles of *satyagraha.* (Even in *Seven Beauties* the photograph of Pasqualino in his home faces a bust of Christ). We recall the earlier "preconcentration camp" Pasqualino, intent on the honor of his seven sisters and his own manliness. Now we see the compromised Pasqualino, bent on survival at any cost. All his sisters, even his wife-to-be, have become prostitutes. The Christ gaze is as judgmental as the eye of the skate-fish at the end of Fellini's *La Dolce Vita.* All three films discussed complement each other neatly to form a cinematic triptych regarding a nonviolent political theology that is universal and non-confessional. For as Gandhi once said: "When selfless activity becomes the motivating factor in one's commitment to humanity, humanity arises." This is the essence of peaceful conflict in the service of liberation. Faith must be embodied in historical expressions that stand in judgment on existing conditions. Paul Tillich's ground of being does not come within the reach of our senses. It must be inferred by example, as with a Sol Nazerman or a Gandhi. God then is mediated as a liberating, supremely loving, and just personal God, not as judge, stern father, moral bookkeeper or, as in James Joyce's experience, "the hangman God."

NOTES

1. For excellent articles on Ozu and his similarity to John Ford's philosophical signature, see Stuart Byron, "The Decline of Consciousness One," *The Village Voice*, January 21, 1971; and Jonathan Cott, "The Art of Ozu," *The Village Voice*, April 13, 1972.

2. See Byron, "Decline."

3. See Jay Cocks, "Painful Accuracy," *Time*, June 4, 1973, p. 44.

4. For a good treatment of John Garfield's screen character, see Joe Morella and Edward Z. Epstein, *Rebels: The Rebel Hero in Films* (New York: Citadel Press, 1971), pp. 5ff.; also H. Gelman, *Films of John Garfield* (New York: Citadel Press, 1976).

5. See the article of Michael Weinstein in *Coercion*, ed. J. Roland Pennock and John Chapman (Chicago: Aldine-Atherton, Inc., 1972), p. 66.

6. See Lawrence Shaffer's excellent review of Coppola's *The Conversation* in *Film Quarterly*, April 1974, pp. 54ff.

2.

The Charismatic Liberator

"Charism" was originally a word used by theologians. Its Greek derivative implied "grace," something unexpected, unpredictable, and outside the routine events of history. Max Weber, the noted German sociologist, secularized the term, extending it to mean the ability of an actor to exercise diffuse influence over the normative, and therefore behavioral, patterns of others. Personal charisma is not achieved, but is a mysterious endowment freely bestowed. It is an uncanny quality in persons that attracts others to submit to their leadership. Since there is inherent drama in such personalities, motion pictures have treated case studies. We recall H. B. Warner as Christ in *King of Kings* (1925), Richard Burton as *Alexander the Great* (1956), Marlon Brando as Marc Antony in *Julius Caesar* (1953), Rod Steiger as Napoleon in *The Battle of Waterloo* (1971), Kirk Douglas as the slave rebel in *Spartacus* (1960), Ingrid Bergman in *Joan of Arc* (1948), Alec Guiness in *Hitler* (1962), Jack Palance in *Che!* (1971), and the documentary about the late President John F. Kennedy, *Four Days in November* (1964). There is no more important element in any liberation model than the leadership role. We have already referred to examples in our film discussions of *Cool Hand Luke* and *Nine Hours to Rama*.

Charisma in a leader can serve to reinforce the interests of an existing power structure, it can purify an institution, or it can help create an alternative lifestyle next to the dominant culture within which it exists. Leni Riefenstahl's *Triumph of the Will* suggested that Hitler was a god whom the German masses would follow to effect a resurrection of the Fatherland which had been crucified at Versailles. This film exemplified totalitarian charism, contrasting with three films of conservative charism *(Lawrence of Arabia*, 1962), of progressive charism *(Brother Sun, Sister Moon*, 1972), and of radical charism *(Woodstock*, 1972). It is important in this discussion of charismatic "liberators" to understand that one group's liberation is necessarily another group's repression. An attractive word, "charism" is thought of as a positive quality. In a science of liberation, it must be seen more neutrally as having its shadow side together with its bright connotation.

David Lean's *Lawrence of Arabia* boasts two stars: Peter O'Toole, in his debut, and the Sahara Desert, magnificently captured in color photography. O'Toole plays T. E. Lawrence, the British archeologist, who by a combination of fortuitous circumstances during World War I became the legendary leader of the Arab tribes. The British, who later made Lawrence a colonel, were interested in resisting the Turks, since they were allied with the Axis powers. Lawrence knew Arabic, could ride camels, could withstand the desert heat, and in general commanded the awesome respect of the Bedouin Arabs. In the film we see Lawrence as a godlike liberator, the famed "El Aurens," as the worshipping Bedouins called him. The life of T. E. Lawrence is controversial. Lowell Thomas, the American reporter, made him a worldwide celebrity, and Lawrence himself wrote a classic called *The Seven Pillars of Wisdom.* The complexity of his character has led to conflicting psychological interpretations of his motives. What seems to have happened is that his consciousness was torn between his scholarly and humanistic training and his new vocation as a military leader. He admits at the end of *The Seven Pillars of Wisdom* that the Arab sense of independence could not lead anywhere and that he acted more as a British officer in organizing Arab resistance against the Turks than as a liberation leader.

This fissure of consciousness was not apparent in his early campaigns where he deliberately avoided bloodshed and concentrated on "hit-and-run" tactics such as blowing up railroad supply lines and then swiftly retreating. However the accumulation of events dulled his refined sensibilities. The fever of conflict, the inevitable loss of Arab lives, pressure by the British to produce swifter results, and his own degradation by a Turkish colonel after being captured—all these events apparently conspired to create in him an appetite for slaughter. The romance of the desert and his role as a sheik were short-lived. The angels of his better nature were overcome by the expediency of battle plans and international diplomacy. When the war ended, he saw the Arab tribes lapse back into their nomadic customs of individual policy-planning and despaired of any united Arab front.

The film poignantly portrays his disillusionment at the outcome of what had begun as a glorious crusade for liberty and self-determination. The Sykes-Picot Treaty between the French and the British tore away the last veil of idealism, and Lawrence realized that his commitment was but a thread in a larger design of geopolitical strategy. A revolutionary leader, Lawrence saw that he was serving Britain's age-old tradition of divide-and-conquer as a means to preserving British imperial interests. Often charismatic liberation leaders and their followers become so enthusiastically identified with their own cause that they lose sight of the other power pieces on the world chessboard of politics. What is an end for one liberation group may prove to be a means for a more powerful vested-interest group. *Lawrence of Arabia* shows the death of Lawrence. Having become a Royal Air Force mechanic, desirous of shunning the spotlight of publicity, Lawrence died in a motorcycle accident, careening off the road rather than colliding with two youths.

Charismatic leaders are generally considered deviants—real or potential—by the organizations they work for. The reason is that they answer to a personal set of motivations that are unpredictable, whereas organizations have routine expectations of their members in order to achieve coordination in the service of collective goals. In his valuable study, *A Comparative Analysis of Complex Organizations*, Amitai Etzioni treats how organizations seek to channel charismatic power, to limit its effect, or to eliminate it, if it proves threatening. In *Lawrence of Arabia*, we saw how the unusual leadership abilities of Lawrence were directed toward the cause of England and only secondarily to serve the Arabs who fought with and under "El Aurens."

Here we wish to study the modification of charismatic behavior through the routinization techniques of integration into large-scale organization. The case of St. Francis of Assisi is not only one of the most remarkable instances of charism in recorded history, but it is also one of the saddest in terms of the cooling of a vision by the very followers of the charismatic "liberator." Franco Zeffirelli directed a film based on Francis's conversion, his gathering of disciples including St. Clare, and his petition to Rome to found a new religious order committed to the twin ideals of strict poverty and universal love. The film was called *Brother Sun, Sister Moon* (1972) in reference to Francis's beautiful Canticle to the Sun.

Played by a young British actor, Graham Faulkner, Francis is seen as rejecting the comfortable upper-class life of his family and aspiring to a life of a mendicant. His spiritual transparency revealed in his direct communion with the elements and animals attracts followers. Together they restore an abandoned church in the countryside and live a life of evangelical simplicity. Francis is not without his enemies who try to cast doubts on the orthodoxy of his radical way of Christian living. In utter faith, Francis insists on making a pilgrimage to Rome in order to have an audience with the pope in the hopes of receiving permission to found a new religious order. Overcoming the bureaucratic difficulties of gaining admission to the pope's audience chamber, Francis and his disciples make a profound impression on Pope Julian II, played by Alec Guiness. The pope is not threatened by the "lovable lunacy" of the mendicants and blesses them, reminding all in his court that there is not only original sin but original innocence as well. The film thus has a "happy ending."

However history tells us that a short while after the death of "Il Poverello," when his stigmatized body was brought on a litter to the tiny Portiuncula in Assisi, his will was burnt. The reason? Francis had charged his followers to remain Gospel-poor. Ironically, to honor the saint of poverty, who some claim was the most Christlike man to have ever lived, funds were collected to build an imposing basilica. The "cooling" of charisma is a well-known phenomenon in the history of religion, and especially Christianity. Sects begin with fervor and enthusiasm, then they grow, and finally comes the routinization of charisma. It becomes predictable, safe, and no longer capable of liberating. Pier Paolo Pasolini's ironic *Hawks and Sparrows* brings out an interesting point, namely that charismatic pacifists are doomed to extinction. His image is of hawks swooping down on the defenseless sparrows and eliminating them. Charisma, even when it does not "cool," can be dampened by the competing forces dictated by the law of the survival of the fittest.

Eisenstein's *Ivan the Terrible* studied a highly contradictory ruler, the Muscovite prince Ivan IV, who united Russia and had himself crowned Tsar. In Part I of Eisenstein's projected trilogy, Ivan is seen as a god, protecting the people; in Part II he is seen beleaguered by the Boyars and his aunt, who plot his downfall. Ivan is seen as human, defensive, and doubting. Part III was never made. The Stalin regime did not like the ambiguity of Ivan's portrayal. Eisenstein had to publish a letter confessing his ideological errors. In 1948 he died; in 1959 *Ivan the Terrible (II)* was released in Paris—an immortal study of autocratic charisma.

An exceptionally intriguing examination of the cooling of charismatic leadership is offered by Hungarian director Miklos Jancsó in *Agnus Dei*. Toward the end of World War I, peasants are roused to revolutionary fervor by a priest who is both epileptic and apocalyptic, a strange combination of mental imbalance and primitive prophecy. Out of the crowd appears an officer who is attracted to the clerical visionary. The officer plays the fiddle (music within the film is a pet technique of Jancsó, adding greater dramatic power than an off-screen soundtrack). He also assists the priest during his fits and seizures. Consequently, the priest devolves charismatic power upon the devoted soldier in a ritual that appears to be a knighthood ceremony. Without warning or psychological preparation for the viewers, the officer takes his gun and shoots the priest. He leaves on a train, now that force has removed the unpredictable source of charismatic leadership.

This "cooling down" of revolutionary fervor is a favorite theme of Jancsó (e.g., *The Red Psalm*, 1971). The freezing of the Russian Revolution within a single decade is another apt case study of this phenomenon. Alexander Solzhenitsyn, in his fictionalized account *Lenin in Zurich*, attributes to the noted revolutionary an imperious urge to go back to Russia in the "sealed train" provided by the German high command and thus remove Russia from the war. Lenin, Solzhenitsyn acknowledged, "was acting in obedience to the power which drew him on." He is pictured as saying on the occasion of the March 1917 revolution: "Suddenly you must climb up to a high place and say: Yes, here I am! Take up your arms, I will lead you!" This was the peak of enthusiasm in the Revolution as depicted in the forties.

The Russian film *Lenin in Moscow* continues where Solzhenitsyn's novel leaves off. After Lenin came Josef Stalin, who would regiment the revolution and continue the revisionism of the teachings of Marx and Engels. Stalin's cruel policies have been amply documented. No western films have as yet attempted to portray Stalin in depth; the Hollywood film *Mission to Moscow* (1943) was made when the U.S.S.R. was a U.S. ally in World War II. The de-Stalinization process came quickly after that leader's death. Will the same happen in Communist China? The towering charismatic stature of Mao Tsetung is convincingly portrayed in an entertaining political suspense film, *The Chairman* (1971), which starred Gregory Peck. Already some "cooling down" has taken place in China. The de-mythologization of Chairman Mao is expected to occur as Chinese leaders seek to accommodate to new conditions. Time trieth truth!

One of the great modern Latin American legends is that of Eva Perón, the actress who as Colonel Juan Perón's wife endeared herself to the masses in Argentina and became known affectionately as Saint Evita. In a Yugoslavian film entitled *Little Mother* (1974), Eva Perón was shown as a shrewd and calculating opportunist who catapulted herself into the role of patroness of the poor and downtrodden, thus entrenching her husband's power as a demagogue. The masses' imperious need for leadership blinds them to the shallow side of the charismatic persona.

Not surprisingly, charisma has a way of perpetuating itself long after the death of the leader. This is particularly the case with working class heroes such as Eva Perón. It is noteworthy that films often portray the "blue collar" class as coarse, manipulable, and even fearful. Certainly the presentation of worker types was not at all flattering in such films of the seventies as *Joe, Straw Dogs, Five Easy Pieces, Easy Rider, Charley Varrick*, and *Taxi Driver*.

However, there are three movies that deal with the martyrdom of men who selflessly devote themselves to the betterment of the lot of workers. In all three films, the leaders were framed with charges for murders that they did not commit: *Sacco and Vanzetti* (1972), *Joe Hill* (1972), and *White Line Fever* (1975). The last named film, unlike the other two, is fictional, but does convey the sense of corruption reaching to high places. In this respect it recalls the powerful semi-fictionalized film, *On the Waterfront*.

In *Sacco and Vanzetti*, shot in Italy, we see a documentary-type recreation of one of the most famous trials in this century. Three issues emerge in the film. First, we see the sincerity of the two anarchist immigrants fighting for a cause they believe in. Their humanity comes to the fore as they recall the image of a comrade plunging to his death from the fourteenth story of police headquarters. The long courtroom trial scenes also give a convincing sense of the psychological pressures on the two defendants. As immigrants and anarchists they become the object of suspicion and hate. Public opinion is definitely against them. Second, the film unmasks the corrupt political system that is intent on crushing the two men in order to preserve the status quo. The letters exchanged between Sacco and Vanzetti reveal their idealism, their faith in themselves and their cause. Third, the film presents us with the theme of immortal symbols—martyrs who become a sign of hope and renewed energy on the part of those who are opposed to injustice.

Bo Widerberg, the Swedish director, separates Joe Hill the man from the legend, which—as the film teaches us—was manipulated by the opportunistic leaders who succeeded Joe Hill. Widerberg makes an important point, namely, how movements with just grievances become fossilized and ideologically rigid. Again adversary situations tend to level rival groups since passion and hate dull the critical intelligence that is indispensable for any true liberation process. As the film ends, complacent union leaders are shown sitting around the table weighing and placing bits of ashes of cremated Joe Hill's body into envelopes to be mailed to locals across the nation. While the ending is weak, striving too much for emotional effect, nevertheless, Joe Hill demonstrates the influence that can be exercised from the grave.

An interesting low budget U.S. film of 1975 was *White Line Fever*, a taut portrayal of an ex-veteran who marries and then buys his own trucking rig to follow in his father's footsteps. He meets with offers involving

smuggling and fraud. His anti-crime position leads to
trouble: He is beaten; his truck is damaged and a
poisonous snake is put in the cab; a friend of his father is
killed and he is charged with the murder; a black trucker
is cruelly killed and left in his bedroom. This sight un-
hinges his pregnant wife who loses their child and is no
longer capable of having any children. The reference to
"shadowy higher-ups" recalls *On the Waterfront.* In a
state of committed rage the hero charges the Glass
House estate where the top boss lives. The truck crashes
dramatically and the driver is injured. The workers
rally around him in a wheelchair outside the hospital.
His wife looks sadly down at him, wondering when he
will learn that his obligations to his family cannot be
sacrificed. *White Line Fever* is good entertainment and
contains several points to illustrate the process of
consciousness-raising and the contagion of charismatic
leadership.

This same effect of immortalizing a martyred leader
appears in Gillo Pontecorvo's film, *Burn!* in which Jose
Dolores is martyred as a rebel at the hands of Sir William Walker. It also pervades Gordon Parks's *Leadbelly*,
the story of Huddie Ledbetter, the legendary prison
blues-singer, king of the twelve-string guitar.[1]

Amitai Etzioni has pointed out how the church can
"turn deviant charismatic symbols into a focus of conforming identification" through the process of canoni-
zation. By reinterpreting the image of the deviant
leader, devotion to the charismatic symbol is rechan-
neled to the organization and its goals—as in the case of
Francis of Assisi, Joan of Arc, Thomas Aquinas, Ig-
natius of Loyola and others, who during their lifetimes
were unquieting influences in the church. The power of
charismatic figures like St. Francis imposes inevitable
strains on organization discipline, for it grants to members a very personalized way of influencing large num-

bers without direct accountability to the organization.

Franco Zeffirelli, the director of *Brother Sun, Sister Moon*, said in an interview that he deliberately cast St. Francis as a hippie, for in his view many of the economically comfortable youth of Europe and North America were like "Il Poverello" involuntarily lowering their standard of living for an idea. In a sense, mendicant orders such as the Franciscans are "countercultures." With its own characteristic lifestyle (i.e., dress, hair, drugs, mobility),the contemporary counterculture has bred many charismatic leaders—often in the form of Indian-beaded, blue-jeaned, long-haired, guitar-playing artists. It started with Elvis Presley and reached its peak with the Beatles, the Liverpudlian quartet that swept the world with a startling new type of music and lyrics that even serious critics had to admit was streaked with true genius. The magnetic appeal of the Beatles was captured brilliantly in Richard Lester's film, *A Hard Day's Night*. Other counterculture idols appeared: Bob Dylan, Joan Baez, Ritchie Haven, Janis Joplin, and combinations with colorful names such as the Jefferson Airplane. Through recordings, audio cassettes, radio, TV, movies, and "live" appearances at rock shrines like Fillmore East, youthful and gifted charismatics helped create a social-normative organization to compete with coercive organizations such as the military establishment, with utilitarian organizations such as the corporations, and with normative organizations such as churches, synagogues, and universities (which were seen as a part of the dominant consumer culture).

The motion picture *Woodstock* (1972) is eminently suitable to illustrate the crowd aspects of counterculture charisma, which has become to a notable degree integrated into the dominant culture. Michael Woodleigh directed *Woodstock*, a cinéma-vérité film composed solely of scenes and footage shot before, during, and immediately after the unprecedented rock-music festival held in 1969 in Woodstock, New York. The audience sees the massive preparations for the "happening" and watches the audience arrive from distant and near places to spend three days seeing and listening to the best of the counterculture's musicians (only Bob Dylan was missed). The film then cuts to the stage and shows us the array of stars from England and America: Joe Cocker, the Who, Joan Baez, Ritchie Haven, Jimi Hendrix, and others. The performances are frenetic as the musicians, realizing that there may never be another audience like this, looked for depths of inspiration worthy of the occasion.

The film is important not only as entertainment, but also as a socio-psychological study in the behavior patterns of those who follow charismatic leaders. Any liberation process must have a "following." The Woodstock devotees came in streams—so many that they broke through the fence surrounding the field and were then permitted to come in without paying. Drugs were consumed freely and an announcement had to be made to warn the audience that some bad L.S.D. was being circulated. As the performers appeared in all their sound and fury, the film cut sporadically back and forth to the audience—a veritable sea of swaying, hand-clapping viewers, ecstatic and often "stoned" on drugs. Young people in crowds often create projections of their imaginary selves, an idealization of what they perceive in the media. (In his study for the University of Toronto Press, *Charisma: A Psychoanalytic Look at Mass Society*, Irving Schiffer, M.D., has discussed how the young are influenced by extra-familial figures of a charismatic nature.)

Woodstock also shows us the aftermath of the "happening." The collective euphoria is quickly dissipated. In its place we see the lonely littered countryside and the abandoned stage. All that remains is the memory. But those who were there will tell you: What a memory! For those who feel that they are a minority or oppressed, moments of escape or of solidarity or of comfort in memories are crucial to support the alien environment that serves as the host organism for their particular subculture—in this case "the hippies." *Woodstock* is a remarkable study of crowd psychology and charismatic inspiration.

It would be rewarding to compare this film to movie studies of Hitler. Richard Basehart's role as the Fuhrer in *Hitler* (1962) is a case in point. We see Hitler in his private life, fallible and feeling. Then his public appearances convert him into another person, a veritable god filled with energy by the enthusiastic Nazi followers who invest him with preternatural power. Leni Riefenstahl's *Triumph of the Will* (1936) recorded faithfully how this power actually manifested itself at the Sixth Congress Party meeting of the Nazis at Nuremberg where there appeared the "goose-stepping" Nazi troops, Adolph Hitler, Goebbels and Goering, and thousands of ecstatic supporters of the Third Reich.

There are those who think that implicit in the "rock" culture portrayed by *Woodstock*, with its liturgies of light, rhythm, and movement, is the same fascist syndrome that served as an engine for National Socialism and its seductive nighttime rallies. The danger of charismatic music idols bringing about a teenage totalitarianism was in fact explored in two remarkable films: Barry Shear's *Wild in the Streets* (1969) and Peter Watkins' *Privilege* (1970). In both films rock 'n' roll stars convert their entertainment talents into political capital as if the music charts were equivalent to polls. The visceral appeal of countercultural charismatics is often enlisted to support political candidates in democracies such as America and England.

The shortcomings of the male charismatic have been brilliantly satirized by Lina Wertmuller in *Love and Anarchy* (1974). The film opens with portraits of Mussolini, Il Duce, with staring eyes and jutting jaw. We meet Spatoletti, head of the security police, blustering and overbearing, and Turin, a peasant bent on assassinating Mussolini. Spatoletti and Turin patronize the same brothel, where "women live in an enforced community without privacy (they are constantly intruding on one another), while their leisure time is poisoned by mutual recriminations and bickering."[2] Turin is attracted to one prostitute, the blonde Salome, who admires his readiness to die for an ideal, but to the dark Tripolina, his political heroics and concerns for justice are irrelevant. ("Justice, my ass! The dead are buried, that's justice.") Tripolina triumphs by having Turin oversleep. Ordinarily passive, he becomes furious and showers her with blows and curses before going out into the street to pursue his anarchic aims. The soldiers kill him, after his refusal to talk under torture. Turin's answer to Spatoletti's question has a thundering humility. When asked, "Who are you?" He answers: "Nobody." Turin dies a political martyr but unsung.

The revolutionary martyrs exercise a power that exceeds their actual deeds. We see this in Latin America with Che Guevara, Camilo Torres, and Salvador Allende. The glorification of these men must be explained in part by the messianic yearning of the oppressed for embodied hope. We need further research on the psychic conditions that prepare the path for liberators, whether assassins or crusaders. Irvine Schiffer's study *Charisma*, while Freudian in approach, is a valuable beginning.

The charismatic female leader deserves attention. Joan of Arc immediately comes to mind and directors return to her time and again: Carl Dreyer's *The Passion of Joan of Arc* (1927), Victor Fleming's *Joan of Arc* (1948), Otto Preminger's *Saint Joan* (1957), and Robert Bresson's *The Trial of Joan of Arc* (1965). Marie Falconetti has earned a niche in the pantheon of cinema acting for her anguished portrayal of the Maid of Orleans in Dreyer's silent classic. Her face spoke volumes. We understand why Joan prefers to die at the stake rather than to betray her "inner voices." A higher imperative is at work and we feel it radiate from the victim.

In Fernando Arrabal's *Guernica* (1976), Mariangela Melato (the Tripolina of *Love and Anarchy)* plays the celebrated Communist leader of the Spanish Civil War, La Pasionaria. She immortalized the boastful war cry: "They shall not pass." ("No pasarán.") In the film she shouts these words from a small cage where she has been imprisoned. Intercut with newsreel footage in sepia, the film recreates the famous assault on Guernica and life in a fortified Basque village, where La Pasionaria takes refuge with her lover rather than seek refuge across the Pyrenees in France. Small wonder that in the hearts of Communists: "La Pasionaria lives!" *Guernica* captures the mystique of comradeship and its sexual equality at the moment when revolutionary sparks are struck from the anvil of a new popular consciousness.

The price of being a charismatic leader is high. The followers rarely live up completely to one's expectations of liberation, as in *Brother Sun, Sister Moon*; the institution or dominant culture never is quite at ease with the "anti-project" or the alternate lifestyle, as in *Woodstock*; and the charismatic actor is tempted to megalomania or overweening ambition, as in *Lawrence of Arabia*. The three films analyzed in this chapter are also complementary in another way, for they show how charism may be exercised at different levels. T. E. Lawrence is an example of the charismatic leader at the top. He kept in touch with the British, it is true, but the Bedouin tribal chieftains looked to Lawrence for their orders and not to the British military commanders. In the case of Francis of Assisi, the charisma was exercised in a position subsidiary to the pope, to whom "Il Poverello" was obedient. The appearance of charism in the ranks other than the top can be exemplified by the motion picture, *Woodstock*, and the inspirational influence that showpeople from the counterculture exercise on the youth of the world. These three movies illustrate liberating charisma at work in the politico-military, the religious, and the socio-economic orders. That is why we feel that these particular films are qualified to support our theses about "the Reel Revolution," that they are generative of crucial lessons for a science of liberation.

In his book *Earthwalk*, Philip Slater makes an important point that is borne out in this chapter, namely, that in the West the use of the word "power" connotes achievement, ambition, and control, whereas in other cultures, "power" is often meant to signify "the ability to influence others, to arouse love and respect, and to get one's needs met without pressure and in a socially naked and unadorned state, devoid of status, position, or other weaponry." Certain charismatic types are forgetful of themselves and refuse to instrumentalize others. T. E. Lawrence, Francis of Assisi, Joan of Arc, La Pasionaria, and the musical "superstars" of the counterculture are opposed to the acquisitive and dominating motives at work in contemporary civilization. They all carry within them some vision that, when translated into verbal and behavioral expressions, resonates in turn in the depths of the being of their followers. There are film studies of the negative effects of charisma, such as those briefly alluded to in this chapter: *Agnus Dei, Lenin In Moscow, The Chairman, Little Mother.*

The charismatic leader must be seen as an ambivalent force, one who starts out by calling forth in those who are disenchanted with bureaucracy and corruption a will to change, a resolve to create institutions and patterns of life closer to the heart's desire. Then the corrosive acids of power and prestige begin to do their work. Over time the routinization of charisma becomes inevitable. The flame must be rekindled, again and again. For the spirit breathes where it will and is constantly stirring the historical waters. If liberation is a recognizable force moving humanity toward a self-realization of its full potential as a freedom-drenched cooperative species, then specially endowed women and men will act as the spark to keep the torch of hope burning. The study of charismatic endowment is ingredient to motion pictures. Witness Walt Disney's ability to weave spells over mass audiences through identification with exceptional, often conformist, animated cartoon heroes who had undeniable charism.[3] Disneyland and Disneyworld epitomize the American way of life.

NOTES

1. See Gordon Parks, "A Last Visit to Leadbelly," *New York Magazine*, May 19, 1976, pp. 66ff.

2. Peter Biskind, "Lina Wertmuller: The Politics of Private Life," *Film Quarterly*, Winter 1974–75, p. 15.

3. More study is needed of the ideological implications of Walt Disney's Mickey Mouse, the Three Little Pigs, and the Three Caballeros. See the article on Aesop on the assembly line in "Father Goose," *Time*, December 27, 1954, pp. 42ff. For a critical Marxist view, see Francisco Pérez, "Walt Disney, una pedagogía reaccionaria," *Cine Cubano* 81, pp. 12–15.

3.

The Degrees of Consciousness-Raising

Paulo Freire, the author of *Pedagogy of the Oppressed*, has cautioned about misinterpreting the Brazilian word *conscientização* as merely "becoming aware" (in French *la prise de conscience*).[1] He brings out the three discriminating moments in the process of consciousness-raising or "conscientization":

1. The awareness of structural guilt, that we are servants of power. Saul Bellow has put it succinctly in his novel, *Dangling Man*, namely, the realization that we are all "guilty of not being innocent."

2. The search for a liberating alternative, what Freire would call an "anti-project." Here one withdraws from any roles of complicity in oppressive structures and searches to work shoulder-to-shoulder with others in the task of humanization.

3. The conversion of the person conscientized into what Freire has called a utopian agent, one who assumes risk and makes a critical commitment to that kind of historical change that is concerned with subhumans, marginal peoples, and the submerged two-thirds of the planet's population.

The three moments discussed by Freire resemble the

instars, or biological growth stages, by which the bright-winged butterfly emerges from the cocoon and the earlier stage of pupa. In each one of us there are surprising potentials. *Larvati prodimus* (Disguised go we forth). Plato knew the soul has wings but, as he knew full well, they must be exercised. I was moved when Daniel Berrigan told a gathering how it gradually dawned upon him that he had to define himself *actively* in the face of America's involvement in a land, sea, and air war in Southeast Asia. If not, said Berrigan, he would be defined by default and against the deepest principles of his being.

The Cuban movie *Lucia* (1968) superbly illustrates Freire's three growth stages of consciousness-raising, anti-project, and alternative action. Directed by Humberto Solas, *Lucia* is composed of three separate periods of Cuban history in which women named Lucia lead quite different lives. The first period, 1895, is that of Cuba's independence from Spain; the second is 1933, or the end of the dictatorial reign of Machado; and the third is the 1960s after the literacy campaign in Castro's post-revolutionary Cuba. A love story stitches the three historical periods together but in ways differentiated by the social class membership of each Lucia. The first Lucia belongs to the landed creole aristocracy; the second pertains to the upper middle class of the depression years; and the last is from what, under Batista's government, would have been the rural peasant class. Solas admitted that each love story, a woman's relationship to a man, reflects a particular society; when taken together the trilogy portrays decolonization, the end of internal exploitation, and finally the spread of communitarian goals with personhood at the core. Solas overlooks the political costs of a police state, but *Lucia* does show the decrease in both physical and social violence in Cuba.

In the 1895 segment we see the opulence, leisure, and shallowness of Havana's elite class, with imported furniture, sculptures, photographs, and drapes. We meet the strange Fernandina, who strikes us as a sort of La Pasionaria. She screams in the street, "The Cubans are sleeping," and at the close she is obviously mad, shouting, "Wake up, Cubans." Lucia, the protagonist, has an affair with a Spanish man of fortune but it ends with betrayal. He uses love to obtain military information; for him love is a tool of political expediency. Fernandina and Lucia murder him in an act of political vengeance. Throughout there are festive activities of Cuba's blacks, the purest cultural element in the new nation. Dancing and black rhythms highlight the influence of that racial strain in Cuban society. It is in the central plaza that people mingle and show their free spirit. In the final scene no one speaks. The director explained this as the loss of language to symbolize a new consciousness as if the Cubans were being born all over again.

The 1933 segment shows us another Lucia who changes her upper-class lifestyle to take a job in a drab cigar factory in Havana. A flashback shows her and her mother going away on vacation while the father remains in the capital city with his mistress. Lucia becomes involved with a rebel fighter, Aldo, who has been wounded in a resistance battle against the cruel Machado government. This radicalizes her; she spurns her past conditioning to become a factory worker in Havana and an activist in workers' demonstrations. Aldo is killed and Lucia is left alone in isolation. Seemingly with hope extinguished, she awaits the birth of her child by Aldo. One reviewer perceptively pointed out: "Nevertheless, the moments of solidarity among the women of the factory show more promise for the future than do Aldo's individualistic and ultimately nihilistic acts."[2]

In *Lucia196–*, Tomás refused to allow his wife Lucia to work. This is the central issue—*machismo*—and presents a sharp contrast with the tragic, turbulent events of the earlier two segments. Havana is no longer the central focus of the film but rather the rural communities. The chief episode is a country-wide literacy campaign. Solas, searching for revolutionary film techniques, uses a grainy film stock, giving the impression of a home-movie seen in a familiar family setting. Farmers and their families are depicted in a determined collective effort to increase crop productivity. There is no more violence as in the 1890s and 1930s but peace and growing prosperity. This last segment focuses on a real problem of male dominance in the patriarchical nuclear family, while immersing the viewer in the new communitarian patterns of solidarity and support.

We should mention here Tomás Gutiérrez Alea's *Memories of Underdevelopment* (1968), another Cuban film released in the United States and listed as one of the New York Film Critics' "Ten Best Films." Sergio lives in post-revolutionary Cuba, or rather he lives alongside of it, nourishing his life by habits of the past—womanizing, wining, and dining. He is an "immigrant in time," that is, a person who feels displaced without changing geographical location. Sergio longs for the fleshpots of Egypt as did the reluctant members of Moses' march through the desert after their miraculous delivery from political bondage. He is a living testimony to the contradictions of Thomas Wolfe's novels: *Look Homeward, Angel!* and *You Can't Go Home Again*. He is a backward-looking citizen of a society with its face squarely pointed away from the past and toward a new future. If in the three segments of *Lucia* we experience dramatically, even romantically, the liberating stages of growth outlined by Paulo Freire, *Memories of Underdevelopment* gives us the negative proof—no awakening, no structural guilt, no "anti-project," and, finally, no alternatives. Sergio has no ideological roots; he is what the Beatles referred to in one of their popular songs as a "Nowhere Man."

If Sergio in *Memories of Underdevelopment* remains opaque in his consciousness of what has transpired around him, Mimi in Lina Wertmuller's *The Seduction of Mimi* (1974), goes beyond the stage of dawning social consciousness, only to slip back into his pre-liberated state. A Sicilian rock quarrier, Mimi is fired for having voted for a Communist and not for a Mafia-supported candidate. He leaves his wife, Rosalia, to go to Turin; he finds work as a metal worker, joins the Communist party, and lives with Fiore, who bears his child. Transferred to a refinery in his own town, he pursues a double life. Mimi tries to avenge his being cuckolded by getting his rival's wife, Amalia, pregnant. Before the entire town, he suggests they exchange babies. On page 56 we see Mimi (Giancarlo Giannini) posturing before the man who cuckolded him just before a Mafia "hit-man" kills Mimi's adversary. Mimi is accused and imprisoned. When he comes out of jail, he is responsible for three families: Fiore and her child, Rosalia and her child, and the six children of Amalia, whom he seduced.

Overwhelmed by these outsized family obligations, he drifts back to his former conforming stage and seeks a job with the Mafia. At the end he is distributing leaflets to the same rock quarriers with whom he worked. Fiore, still a passionate political activist of the left, scorns him and drives away in a small red truck that carries the emblem of the hammer and sickle. *The Seduction of Mimi* is a searing study of aborted social consciousness.

Mimi imagines himself being persecuted by the Mafia chief (with the menacing three moles on the cheek), symbol of an external fate he cannot escape, but in reality "it is evident that Mimi's delusions of persecution are an externalization of his own voluntary but unexamined choices."[3] Lina Wertmuller depicts the contradictions of Marxism, the Mafia, Christianity, and Communism.[4]

There are "nay-sayers" who are peripheral to society, those who go their own way, who serve the role of latter-day gurus. In their archaic simplicity, they mirror urban-industrial society back to itself so that it can see the dirt on its own face. Chaplin was the "nay-sayer," par excellence. The French comedian, Jacques Tati, is another remarkable, if less celebrated, mime. Although he too is unable to change society, he (like Chaplin) refuses to be changed by it. The audience identifies with Tati despite his role as inevitable "loser" —that is, by society's definition of who a loser is.

Jacques Tati is a comedian in the classic mime tradition of Charlie Chaplin, Buster Keaton, and Harry Langdon.[5] All are noncomformists, skillfully using silent humor as the Archimedean point upon which to rest the lever of their social critique. Like his predecessors, Tati has opposed the depersonalized, predictable world of urban-industrial society, that universe without individuality, without responsibility, without love. Tati qualifies for what Paulo Freire would call a "utopian agent." Remaining unaffected by the changes around him, Tati's celluloid puppet, Monsieur Hulot, is quietly different. He is gauche, giraffe-like, and mechanical in his movements. However, gradually, we become convinced that he is more human than the seemingly normal people who, beneath their surface movements, are really automata programmed to the complex rhythms of

Giancarlo Giannini in Lina Wertmuller's The Seduction of Mimi

the machine age. No one has more clearly denounced the consumer society with its cult of efficiency, comfort, and speed than Tati. Not since Chaplin's *Modern Times* did the screen have such a trenchant and humorous critique of contemporary lifestyle as *Monsieur Hulot's Holiday* (1955), an undeniable cinema classic, in which Tati was writer, director, and actor.

As we meet Tati's Monsieur Hulot, the tall vacationer is driving in a fragile "egg-crate" motor vehicle to a beach in Brittany to exploit those precious days that *homo urbanus* needs each year to replenish spent energies. We identify with the awkward child-man who mingles certain traits of Don Quixote, Francis of Assisi, and Peter Pan. There is no plot to the film—merely a series of incidents, all sight gags. Hulot is the only one who is spontaneous and ready to risk. He looks like a self-winding toy soldier, awkward in his angular movements. However, we soon learn to see how vital he is in contrast to his fellow vacationers: the secretary who poses in her bathing suit and tries to dissimulate her boredom, the middle-aged couple resigned to their shared life of "quiet desperation," the retired army officer who relives and retells military battles of the past, the conservative English dowager, the hotel manager and the bus boy.

If, as Norman Cousins once contended, modern man is obsolete, then perhaps the most telling symptom of this can be found in the contemporary patterns of recreation and vacationing. It is curious how many people travel hundreds, even thousands, of miles to bathe in suntan lotion and expose themselves to sun without entering the ocean they have so eagerly and expensively sought out. *Monsieur Hulot's Holiday* is a highly significant denunciation, even though quiet, of the contemporary use of leisure. Nothing is more publicized and commer-

cialized than vacation, that "time in parenthesis."
However, critical reflection reveals that this short-term
lease on pleasure is a mirage dissipated by means of the
same monotony and routine that the vacationer must
return to. Jacques Tati's Hulot is what David Riesman
has termed an "inner-directed" man, marching to the
beat of his own drum, with no human respect for what
others think. He does not allow himself to be defined by
the expectations of others. In this he is far more liberated than Marcello, the star of Federico Fellini's *La
Dolce Vita*, who marches in lock step with those around
him, all the while knowing that he is an accomplice of a
culture that alienates and debases those whom it is
supposed to nurture. Whereas Marcello cannot find the
strength to risk the disapproval of his peers, Monsieur
Hulot is totally oblivious of their values, their priorities.
He entertains no self doubts; he has existential trust in
life and does not need polls to tell him the direction of the
masses.

Tati's "consciousness-raising" has spanned the
gamut of work (*The Big Day*, 1953), suburbia (*My Uncle*,
1963), leisure (*Playtime*, 1967), and commuting and
travel (*Traffic*, 1972), in addition to his masterly satire
on vacationing in *Monsieur Hulot's Holiday*. In his later
movies, Hulot appears with pipe, raincoat, multi-colored
Argyle socks, and Tyrolean hat *sans* feather. The core of
Tati's philosophy seems to be the belief that spontaneity
is diminishing, that corporate competition inhibits individual initiative, that mechanization is winning the
day. He conveys the distinct impression that people are
having less and less fun. The better angels of our nature
are not being allowed to show themselves. Tati, like
Chaplin and Keaton, wins the audience's sympathies
because he gives witness to more authentic, if less affluent, lifestyles. Hulot is a social misfit, undoubtedly.

Nevertheless, he appears as a majority of one because his sensitivity, his warmth, his love of people make him more real than the statistical majority of so-called normal people who surround him.

Tati is what someone has called an "über-marionette," whose stiff mechanical movements make him more convincing, more desirable than the less human counterparts who regard him as a nuisance. Hulot is like an exile from some other existence, sent on a mission to subvert our rational, conscious patterns, denouncing by his presence the costs of our bureaucratic organizations with their specialized roles, their impersonal chains of command, and their codes of amorality. In *Monsieur Hulot's Holiday*, Tati opens the door of consciousness so that the audience can see that he is not the mechanical puppet he appears to be but rather that the other vacationers are, at bottom, grotesque marionettes moved by invisible wires. Like the prophets, Tati too sows the seeds for the ruin of inauthentic life and calls us to repentance and to rebirth—in the spirit.

One of the greatest social realism films to emerge from Hollywood was Elia Kazan's *On the Waterfront* (1954). Based on Budd Schulberg's script and with the help of Marlon Brando at the peak of his acting career, *On the Waterfront* illustrates all three stages of the "conscientization" process: (1) critical awareness; (2) the construction of an "anti-project" to denounce the evil structure; and (3) historical commitment in terms of confrontation and personal suffering. In the chapter "Peaceful Liberation" we discuss those organizations that have the characteristics of asylums, in which the individual is cared for completely with very little self-determination. Authoritarian labor unions reveal many of the traits of such totalized institutions. *On the Waterfront* is a study of personal and group liberation within the longshoremen's union of New York City. As one of the shoremen's union of New York City. As one of the world's greatest ports, New York has been plagued for generations with corruption on the piers. Budd Schulberg's screenplay, as mentioned in the Introduction, was inspired by the work of the waterfront priest, Father John M. Corridan, S.J., who tried to organize the stevedores and dock workers to resist the collusive exploitative tactics of corrupt union leaders and shipping owners. (In the film, there is a reference to "Mr. Big," a shipping magnate who is alluded to in terms of a shadowy presence as the power behind the longshoremen's leaders.)

Marlon Brando plays Terry Molloy, an ex-prizefighter, who threw a fight on the orders of his brother (Rod Steiger), a henchman of the corrupt union leader, enacted by Lee J. Cobb. Powerful of physique but dull of wit, Terry Molloy meets a lovely college girl (Eva Marie Saint), the daughter of a dock worker and the sister of a murdered stevedore who opposed the tyrannical union bosses. The abstract ideals of justice and gospel liberation, preached by the "waterfront priest" (Karl Malden), make little impact on Terry, although the other longshoremen, outraged by the cruel death of a colleague, are ready to do battle. As Terry falls in love with the sister of the victim, he gradually becomes involved—first emotionally and then intellectually. Persons lead him to principles. The agonizing conflict of allegiances is due to the pleas of the girl that he take a stand of conscience. The priest also appeals to his better nature. Concerned by Terry's wavering loyalty, the union boss warns Terry's brother to handle the matter—either convince him to be loyal, totally and unconditionally, or to eliminate him. The conversation between the two brothers in a car is one of the most moving and superbly acted scenes in the history of movies. Terry looks pitifully at his brother and recalls the night he asked him to throw the fight that could have led to a crack at the world championship. With a heart-breaking expression of regret, Terry whimpers: "I could'uv been somebody." It is the complaint of wasted potential, of lost alternatives.

When the brother refuses to kill Terry, he himself is offered up as a sacrifice. This is the turning point in Terry's life. He becomes committed and gives testimony to the investigating committee regarding the system of exploitation: the "blacklists," the "shape-ups," and the "kickbacks." In Schulberg's original script, Terry Molloy dies. Hollywood, always sensitive to audience reaction and the catharsis of the "happy ending," lets him live. The final scene features a brutal confrontation in a cargo warehouse with a bloody beating that Terry survives. *On the Waterfront* depicts for us the self-awareness of Terry Molloy that grows with the help of the priest and the girl he loves; it depicts his refusal to heed his brother's warning and finally his decision to convert this "anti-project" of independent action into legal testimony that would serve to improve conditions on the piers.

Reformism is the preferential route that most Hollywood films take. *On the Waterfront* is an example. The workers can rebel, but basically they can produce only incremental change. Kazan generally shows lack of belief in any serious effort to change institutional structures—whether the oppressive agricultural system in *Viva Zapata!* or the corrupt political, military, and commercial forces personified in *A Face in the Crowd* (based on Budd Schulberg's exposé of nationwide TV), or government disregard of the interests of residential families displaced for purposes of building a hydroelectric plant in *Wild River*.

The Best Years of Our Lives (1946) studied the efforts of three returning veterans to find as much meaning in their civilian lives as they had in resisting the Japanese and Germans during World War II. This highly success-ful and very sentimental film takes place in a typical heartland American town, Boone City. This town is in a troubled mood—which is never critically examined. Rather our attention is drawn to three personal psychodramas: of an ex-banker (Frederic March), an ex-soda jerker (Dana Andrews), and a paraplegic (Harold Russel). Never is a searching examination made of the institutional forces and social pressures that prevent the returning G.I.'s from finding purpose in life.

Likewise drift and paranoia pervade U.S. films of the seventies: *Shampoo, Nashville, Taxi Driver,* and *All the President's Men.* While the films show some flair for documentary-type realism, they move the audience to-ward no serious collective action as do such films as Costa Gavras's *State of Siege,* Gillo Pontecorvo's *Battle of Algiers,* Solanas and Getino's *Hour of the Furnaces,* Miklos Jancsó's *The Red and White,* Andrej Wajda's *Canal,* Jean Luc Godard's *La Chinoise,* Lina Wert-muller's *Love and Anarchy,* and Satyajit Ray's *The Mid-dleman.* Foreign films as a rule show greater critical vigor and powers of social indignation than U.S. motion pictures, though the films of such U.S. directors as Fre-deric Wakeman, Peter Davis, Brian De Palma, and Shir-ley Clarke do tease audiences into thinking about the inequities of U.S. social existence. As a rule, however, box-office pressures lead to entertainment values, necessarily muting social criticism and promoting ac-ceptance of things as they are.

Freire has said that "the true humanization of man cannot be brought about in the interiority of our minds; it has to take place in external history." While that is true, the transformation of institutions and structures must begin by ceasing to see reality through the veils of the existing values and dominant power relationships. The imagination must be allowed to envision alternatives. Some will be of an absolute utopian nature (that is, unattainable); others will be of a relative utopian character (within reach). Paulo Freire and liberation theologians such as Gustavo Gutiérrez want the theological imagination to be applied to socio-historical realities and not merely to "other-wordly" activity. The world's injustices and evils need not be supported passively in the hopes of compensation in the next life.[6] Paulo Freire wrote to a theology student: "There is no hope in passivity, in accommodation, in making compromises, but rather in the dialectic of restlessness/ peace, which characterizes the critical act of constant searching. My waiting *(espera)* makes sense only if I struggle and seek with hope *(esperanza)*."

In the films discussed in this chapter, there were different degrees of intensity regarding struggle and hope. In *Lucia*, the hope was indeed long-suffering and covered a span of over sixty-five years of Cuban history, from 1895 through the 1933 overthrow of Gerardo Machado to the literacy campaign instituted by Fidel Castro after his defeat of Fulgencio Batista. Though the progression of liberation was evident in terms of greater equality, the film still indicated further advances that would have to be made—explicitly, greater self-determination for women, and implicitly (due to political constraints on artists), greater pluralistic expression and dissent.

In *Memories of Underdevelopment* and *The Seduction of Mimi*, we had two splendid cinematic case studies of still-born consciences. Sergio in the Cuban movie was never impregnated with the seed of revolutionary fervor, while Mimi in Wertmuller's film was, at first, bent on activism in a historical project. However, his tribal ties to family prevented any real embodiment of purpose. The paralysis of the will to work for collective goals is too common a phenomenon. The imperious needs of the ego submit to reason and will only with difficulty. There is a brilliant scene in Lina Wertmuller's *Everything Ready, Nothing Works* (also called *All Screwed Up*). The camera swoops down on the bustle and banter in a restaurant kitchen. A bomb is thrown; arrests are made; all comes to a deathly standstill in the kitchen. What will happen? The thought is suggested to the audience: Why not stop working and look for some more human alternative? We see the workers stare off screen. Will the revolutionary invitation be acted upon? The suspense is taut. Then someone cries out that people in the restaurant want to be served. The spell is broken, the old work habits reassert themselves. The cooks, waitresses, and busboys dash about. Wertmuller's film dramatically portrays the crossroads at which Italy stands in the late seventies—business as usual (with food riots, strikes, and police control) or a new social arrangement.

In *All Screwed Up* the degree of relative deprivation was not intense enough to trigger revolt. As consciousness is raised, tolerance for injustice must be lowered. Also, no dynamic leader emerged to channel the mass dissatisfaction that the prior scenes of chaos evidenced. Wertmuller's films betray a troubled optimism, prefiguring structural changes but at the cost of violence, certainly psychological and probably physical as well.

This troubled optimism is missing in Tati and Kazan, whose films reveal the warts of urban-industrial societies. Tati is a personal rebel by his choice of lifestyle. Terry Molloy in Kazan's *On the Waterfront* resists within the union organization. Lina Wertmuller, on the other hand, is scrutinizing the symbols of motivation and meaning in Italy's dominant Christian culture and its Marxist proletarian subculture. She is loosening the century-old assumptions that have blocked off any thought of a new path of social change which is neither an excessive "property-and-profit" consciousness nor a blind commitment to authoritarian socialist solutions. As all great artists, she is exploring a new area of sensibilities and readying Western audiences for hitherto untried alternatives and social experimentation. Lina Wertmuller and her country, Italy, are to be watched in the coming decade for new patterns of social change. In the West mass media such as movies are infrequently used as instruments of social change. Jean Luc Godard, Gillo Pontecorvo, Costa Gavras and now the brilliant Lina Wertmuller are exceptions to the Hollywood formula of escapism and the "happy ending." Her *Seven Beauties* shows the high human costs of survival.

NOTES

1. See the valuable booklet *Paulo Freire*, in the LADOC "Keyhole" Series, a publication of Division for Latin America, USCC, Box 6065 Washington, D.C. 20005. On page 3 of this study, Freire's meaning of the word "conscientization" is carefully explained.

2. Anna Marie Taylor's review of *Lucia* in *Film Quarterly*, Winter 1974–75, p. 57.

3. See Peter Biskind, "Lina Wertmuller: The Politics of Private Life," *Film Quarterly*, Winter 1974–75, p. 13.

4. Neil Hurley, "Film: Lina Wertmuller as Political Visionary," *The Christian Century*, August 17–24, 1977, pp. 726–28.

5. Walter Kerr, *The Silent Clowns* (New York: Alfred A. Knopf, 1975).

6. Ted Robert Gurr, *Why Men Rebel* (Princeton: Princeton University Press, 1970), p. 24; also O. Mannoni, *Prospero and Caliban: The Psychology of Colonization* (New York: Frederick A. Praeger, 1968), pp. 76ff.

4.

Violence and Liberation

The Bible tells us there is a time for peace and a time for war. History teaches the same lesson. The vast role of violence in this century's history is unarguable. Interesting enough, many wars have religious origins. This is ironic since religion stresses reconciliation, forgiveness, and fraternity. However, religion is one of the most vital components in our ego make-up so that we feel defensive, indeed even righteous, when it is attacked or imperiled.

Otto Preminger's film based on Leon Uris's *Exodus* (1960) is an excellent cinema treatise on violence in the service of religious conviction. A group of European Jewish émigrés run the British blockade at Cyprus and make for Haifa where they are greeted enthusiastically by Palestinian Jews. Paul Newman and Sal Mineo play Israeli freedom fighters while Lee J. Cobb incarnates the role of Ben Gurion. The viewer is drawn into the plot as the Irgun, the Jewish guerrilla movement, cooperates valiantly in the creation of the new state of Israel in 1948—the first Jewish sovereignty since the conquest of Jerusalem by Titus in A.D. 70. *Exodus* is a suspense-action blockbuster, which pleads the case of auto-determination and justifies guerrilla tactics—unusual for Hollywood in the sixties, when the Vietnam war was in progress.

Two silent classics provide us with contemporary case studies of how violence has been used in historical situations to answer injustice: D. W. Griffith's *Birth of a Nation* (1915) and Sergei Eisenstein's *Potemkin* (1925). Both directors, one an American and the other a Russian, helped to write the lexicon of cinema. Griffith introduced film grammar (e.g., the wipe, the dissolve, the fade and the cut), while Eisenstein later showed how clever juxtaposition of scenes could trigger ideas in the minds of the audience (e.g., editing, montage, and a theory of cine-dialectics). The world was stunned first by *Birth of a Nation* and then a decade later by *Potemkin* as both directors used motion to generate emotion and social humanism. In their use of the camera image, both wrote history with lightning by freeing their audiences from the conventional manner of viewing reality. In all the surveys taken both films figure among the ten greatest motion pictures ever made and are often shown at film museums, on campuses, in art theatres and revival programs.

Birth of a Nation and *Potemkin* deal with violence and social change. Griffith chose to study the agonies of racial conflict in the post-Appomattox South, while Eisenstein focused on a sailors' mutiny on the Russian battleship *Potemkin* in the 1905 Revolution. It is noteworthy that irrationality is the seedbed of violence. In Griffith's study of the Civil War it is the Ku Klux Klan that tries to save the Southern way of life from Northern beliefs of emancipation and from what Southerners saw as anarchic black rule. By contrast, Eisenstein portrays the tyranny of Czarist rule and spontaneous rebellion of the *Potemkin*'s crew. Griffith's aristocratic plantation owners represent a traditional social grouping from which life has ebbed; Eisenstein's mutineers represent an amorphous mass of life seeking a new form. In both film masterpieces there are identifiable social biases: *Birth of a Nation* defends tradition and the Southern ante-bellum way of life (Griffith was from Kentucky and his father rode with the Klan), and *Potemkin* argues eloquently the cause of the Bolshevist Revolution. While the translation of these biases into motion picture images was unconscious in each case, the contribution to a science of liberation was quite objective. Violence is a matter of emotion, of subliminal urges and social conditioning. Let us study in more detail the lessons of liberation contained in these two films, which remain unsurpassed for depicting violence amid rapid social changes.

Birth of a Nation imprints its message on the viewer by means of five symbols. As Griffith shows us the Civil War and the silent corpse-strewn battlefield, the subtitle induces an ironic shock: "War's Peace." The aftermath of the war is portrayed in such a way as to enlist the sympathies of the audience. "The Little Colonel," disillusioned, returns to his plantation, a shadow of its earlier prosperity. The South is impoverished and humiliated. The third scene is that of Lincoln's assassination with John Wilkes Booth's cry as he leapt to the stage of the Ford Theatre in Washington, D.C.: *Sic semper tyrannis* (freely translated: "Such is the fate of tyrants"). Griffith takes the viewpoint of the post-Appomattox South—a reason why the film was severely criticized for its partisanship. Following the president's death, Griffith shows us the invasion of carpetbaggers and insolent northern Negroes. The searing image for the rape of the South is the dramatic scene in which the Southern belle, Flora, chooses to plunge from a precipice rather than be raped by a former slave. The fifth and final scene is the triumphal procession of the white-hooded horsemen of the Ku Klux Klan. This scene offsets the earlier one of Sherman's march to the sea. After its premiere in New York City, *Birth of a Nation* was re-edited to mute Griffith's interpretative biases. Southerners maintained that censorship would have not occurred if the premiere had taken place in Atlanta.

A penetrating reaction to this movie classic can be found in James Baldwin's *The Devil Finds Work*. Here Baldwin gives a close analysis of the not-too-subtle editorializing of the central event in U.S. history. Blacks appear either as malevolent schemers and looters or as dependent, faithful "darkies." Fortunately, there are excellent consciousness-raising movies about American blacks *(The Autobiography of Jane Pittman, Sounder, The Great White Hope)*, about Caribbean blacks *(Burn!, Memories of Underdevelopment, Lucia, The Harder They Come)*, and Africans *(Too Late the Phalarope, Something of Value, Come Back, Africa, Zulu,* and *Black and White in Color)*. As an ethnic group, blacks provide rich studies of exploitation, discrimination, and a will to survive with their cultural heritage and identity intact.

Potemkin also has five recognizable segments with corresponding symbols. First, Eisenstein etches with poignant details the oppressive conditions aboard the Russian battleship. The men try to sleep in their hammocks in a sweltering hold. When they awake and are ready to eat, we are shown a close-up of the maggots in their food. Inscribed on the plate is the phrase from the Lord's Prayer: "Give us this day our daily bread!" A bearded Russian priest, the ship's chaplain, brandishes a Byzantine crucifix, urging the men to be content with their lot. In the second segment, the sailors protest and are arrested for mutiny. A tarpaulin is thrown over them as they are huddled together on the deck to be shot. When one appeals to his comrades to join them in the mutiny, the firing squad turns on their superiors.

The mutiny succeeds, but at the cost of the life of the rebel leader. The third segment shows the corpse being brought to shore at Odessa to be buried. The townspeople greet the mutineers sympathetically. They too mourn the dead leader. The subtitle is emotionally-charged as in Griffith's film. It reads: "For a spoonful of soup."

In the fourth segment the Czar's troops arrive to quell the mutiny. The townspeople flee down the Odessa steps that lead to the sea as the troops with rifles drawn advance relentlessly, shooting innocent bystanders. This is undoubtedly the most famous scene in motion picture history. A woman's eyeglasses are shattered by a bullet. It recalls the final scene of *Godfather I*, when a Mafia leader on the massage table is shot and his eyeglasses break, an obvious tribute to Eisenstein. A mother is shot and the baby carriage she was holding bounces down the stairs; a legless beggar uses his arms to flee from the Czar's soldiers who massacre the frightened bystanders indiscriminately. Whereas *Birth of a Nation* showed the Klan as the liberators of the defeated South, *Potemkin*, in its fifth segment, assigns this role to the white-uniformed sailors. As another ship approaches the *Potemkin* we expect a battle. Suddenly the crew of the Czar's ship lets loose a cry of fraternal solidarity, showing that they are joining with the mutiny of the *Potemkin*. Victory and exaltation punctuate the theme of universal brotherhood—a prelude to the Communist overthrow of the Kerensky government in 1917 and Eisenstein's famous silent film *October*.

The same cine-dialectics are present in both *Birth of a Nation* and *Potemkin*. Griffith and Eisenstein are clearly propagandists: the latter upholding the vision of a socialist state in which private property would be absent; the former lamenting the passing of the paternalistic Southern social order with its racial caste system. Curiously, neither director was an advocate of an open social system with equal opportunity for all. The violence we see in their films is one in the service of an ideology. The importance of both films, apart from their deserved niche in the pantheon of silent film art, is in illustrating what Karl Mannheim has termed utopian thinking and conservative ideological thought. Violence is generally the outcome of a clash between two groups divided into utopian and ideological advocates. In *Birth of a Nation*, the blue forces of the North represent a threat to the traditional Southerners, such as Griffith, who saw change as negative. In actuality, the gray uniforms of the South under Robert E. Lee symbolized the feudal heritage of the South with its caste system. In *Potemkin*, the sailors and their civilian sympathizers on the Odessa mainland stood for revolutionary change, as opposed to the Czar and his supporters who were bent on crushing utopian schemes. Griffith and Eisenstein had prescriptions for society and sanctioned violence as a means to attain their respective ideals. There should be more film research regarding the social philosophies of these renowned directors, about whom it could be said that each time we see a movie we see something of the visual and conceptual techniques which each pioneered.

In the United States we have been conditioned by the secular liberation model of democracy, with its stress on a free press, public opinion, minority rights, and consensus mechanisms. It is noteworthy that the underlying social philosophies of *Birth of a Nation* and *Potemkin* betray little sympathy with the secular-libertarian model of freedom and government, which most Americans accept too uncritically. Both Griffith and Eisenstein concurred in their option of a closed society with total allegiance to the ruling elite. By birthright, Griffith defended an agrarian, slave-holding society ruled by genteel aristocrats, while Eisenstein heralded the new autarchy of the masses with the Communist Party as their privileged ruling class and interpreter of historical materialism. Let us contrast these views with a remarkable semi-documentary about American political life and protest in the late sixties.

Haskell Wechsler's *Medium Cool* (1969) is an original look at the 1968 Democratic Convention in Chicago, marked by the protests of the yippies and the hippies. The conflict portrayed in *Medium Cool* is based on a broader notion of violence, namely, institutional violence. Dom Helder Camara, the well-known Brazilian bishop, has said that violence is a three-step process: Institutional violence leads to frustration and physical violence as an attempt at institutional change. This in turn leads to repressive violence. The fact is that violence is a relative concept and embraces not only guerrilla warfare, street fighting, and kidnapping, but also loans at exorbitant interest rates, the concentration of privileges in certain social classes and vested interest groups, and economic coercion.[1] A lyric by Woody Guthrie, whose life was admirably represented by David Carradine in *Bound for Glory*, summarizes poetically this difference in forms of violence:

> As through this world I've rambled
> I've seen lots of funny men
> Some rob you with a sixgun
> and some with a fountain pen.

The importance of *Medium Cool* for this study of violence is that it complements the study of physical violence with a dramatic portrayal of establishment violence, or what has been called "white violence," produced by intricate and invisible structural relationships of oppression.

The sanctions for violence are many, for no one

gratuitously endorses its use.[2] There is always a reason, either conscious or unconscious. However the good reasons offered are not always the real ones which motivate those who use evil. In America there is a sporadic but sustained pattern of violence as if the social system needed it as a deterrence to change or overthrow. Several studies on the roots of violence in America indicate that it lies deep in the national psyche.[3] Certainly the rash of violent movies since 1968 (*Bonnie and Clyde, The Wild Bunch, Easy Rider*) would seem to confirm the curious mass appetite which our advanced industrial society creates for vicarious forms of murder, mayhem, and more recently, masochism. One thinks of such recent films as *Death Wish, Magnum Force, Lipstick, Taxi Driver,* and *The Marathon Man.* Cinema heroes begin to step outside the law: Gene Hackman's Popeye Doyle in *The French Connection,* Charles Bronson in *The Mechanic,* Burt Reynolds in *Hustle,* Steve McQueen in *Bullitt,* Frank Sinatra in *The Detective,* and Clint Eastwood in *Dirty Harry.*

Professor Stanley Milgrim of Yale University has shed considerable, if disturbing, light on the propensity of the average American to inflict violence on another if it is done within the context of an institutional mandate.[4] Dr. Milgrim recruited volunteers who were paid to administer varying levels of electrical shock to a person connected to cathodes. Though the person was also an accomplice of Dr. Milgrim and received no pain, the "guinea pig" volunteers believed they were hurting the subject. Despite protests, some 60 percent of the volunteers cooperated with orders, rationalizing their behavior on the premise that someone else assumed the responsibility. We know that at the Nuremberg trials Nazi war criminals were not allowed to use the argument that they were only acting under orders from superiors. Marcel Ophuls's *Memories of Justice* pointed up how evil could be sanctioned under Hitler just as he also documented in *The Sorrow and the Pity* the conformism of French collaborationists with the repressive Vichy government.

The 1968 Democratic National Convention brought out clearly three forms of institutional (white) violence that many unreflecting citizens fail to include in their condemnations of mugging, looting, burning, and armed protest. The most obvious form portrayed in *Medium Cool* is police brutality. There is a presumption that if uniformed law enforcement officials are exerting violence on civilians, they must have a valid reason. This presumption can be seen in most movies, TV programs, and pulp stories which deal with cops and detectives.

The second form of institutional violence documented in *Medium Cool* is political bossism, that is, the manipulation of democratic principles by special interests. The allusion to Mayor Richard Daley's machine-type politics, even if indirect, is evident in Wechsler's remarkable film.

The last form of institutional violence is the power of media such as television to shape opinion and mold public sentiment. True, *Medium Cool* eloquently argues that TV is a democratic catalyst. However, reflection upon the medium as it exists in the United States shows that it is not only, to use Marshall McLuhan's expression, a "cool medium" but also a "commercial medium." In other words, it is the chief propaganda instrument in the creation of a "consumer society." Economists like John Kenneth Galbraith have aptly pointed out how contemporary western industrial society would be unthinkable without television as a marketing force. "Live" news is irresistible entertainment. While it serves the ideals of democratic expression and news-gathering, it also strengthens the same economic system that undergirds our political system. *Medium Cool*, as most products of a profit-motivated media system, stopped short in its complete analysis of the 1968 Democratic National Covention. In a crucial scene we see soldiers of the National Guard ready to contain the hippies and the yippies. The inequality of power is suggested by the rebel figure in the foreground with an auto tire. TV won sympathy for such "underdogs."

The three films we have treated in this chapter on violence not only make political statements but they refer to the dependence of political acts of violence on economic interests. Karl Marx was the first to relate in systematic form economics, class interest, and political power. One need not accept his theories of surplus value, bourgeois exploitation of the worker class, and the vanishing of the state into a classless, conflict-free society in order to affirm the influence that economics has on political society.

In the slave-holding South, economic interests were involved, especially as technologies like the cotton-gin made cheap slave labor superfluous. Griffith's *Birth of a Nation* is an ideological defense of violence on behalf of a traditional society with undeniable values threatened with the breakup of the ante-bellum Southern way of life.[5] Eisenstein's *Potemkin* is a masterly paean to violence on behalf of a new social order closer to the just demands of the Russian people. The privileges of the upper class and the Czarist court required as a precondition a broad base of agricultural serfs, illiterate and unquestioning in their obedience. In *Medium Cool*, economic interests are not treated explicitly. Nonetheless, a consumer market society bent on expanding psychological wants is the subtext for the film. The United States generally looks at its problems as those of citizens, certain aggrieved groups, or political parties with different platforms on issues. Rarely is the economic system looked at critically as a source of the institutional violence at work. Rather there is a tendency to blame the powerless, the poor, and the prestige-free strata of society.

The recourse to violence inevitably means a reciprocal spiral in which each side escalates its aggressive tacks in a kind of galloping inflation where demand always outruns supply. Gillo Pontecorvo's *The Battle of Algiers* (1966) is an apt film for study in this regard. The French Colonel Mathieu and the Algerian militant Djafor oppose one another in a deathly struggle. Destruction breeds destruction: The National Liberation Front plants bombs and wreaks havoc in strategic locales; the French send in paratroopers to round up suspects and to corral the leaders whose whereabouts are learned through torture. Symbolically, Colonel Mathieu dons dark glasses whenever he issues cruel orders, as if he knows he must cut off the sunny side of his human nature.

There can be a judicial basis to violence, one that appears fair and civilized but is in reality only an exercise of arbitrary power by the irrational social beast. In the Yugoslavian film *Tri* (1966), we have a *tri*-logy that shows how murder can be cloaked in the guise of order. The first vignette shows Yugoslavian soldiers searching a train station during World War II for partisan spies. A man with a camera is apprehended as a suspect; he pleads innocent and insists that he is waiting for his wife and child. When they do not appear, he is summarily shot. Then the dead man's wife and child appear, attesting posthumously to the truth of his claim. In a second segment, one of two fleeing partisans is imprisoned in a straw hut which is set afire. The other refuses to be shot in the back by the firing squad and keeps turning around to face his executioners; they are impatient with this rebellious gesture and shoot him. In the last story, a woman is taken at a farm and tried by a kangaroo court for collaborating. She is marched away to face her death.

Several futuristic films show how violence can be a release from boredom: Jean Luc Godard's *Alphaville* (1966), Giermo Petri's *The Tenth Victim* (1969), Norman Jewison's *Rollerball* (1975), and Stanley Kubrick's *Clockwork Orange* (1972). A brilliant cinematic example of the seductive power of violence is Pascal Aubier's *The Goodbye Singing (Le Chant du Départ*, 1975). Seven members of a lonely Hearts Club meet each week for a meal. All lead lives of quiet desperation in routine "dead-end" positions. A curious telepathic current begins to unite them. With each meal they become friendlier, more trusting, and propose a Sunday picnic. During the week, one member distributes submachine guns and rifles. All are impressed by the firearms. To celebrate the events, a former singer, on request, sings a tender ballad. At noon the next Sunday, they return to the picnic spot. Armed to the teeth, each one says farewell. Embraces are exchanged, and then begins the mutual carnage as a primal scream is heard off screen and ink stains run down the screen. *The Goodbye Singing* touches a hidden chord in the viewer. Violence can be escape, ecstasy.

In closing, we can say that any judgment on violence must be made in function of the context. Edmund Burke, the noted Whig politician and philosopher, defended the American Revolution as a legitimate defense of liberties that were being violated by the British under King George III. However, he vigorously opposed the French Revolution as an anarchic type of protest against undeniable abuses by the nobility and the French king. Theorists such as Karl Mannheim, on the other hand, would see a thinker such as Burke as a historical conservative, over-protective of property interests and the free enterprise economic system. In brief, the position on the left is more critical of institutional violence and more indulgent regarding the use of physical violence as a means of redressing grievances. Those on the right of the ideological spectrum are quicker to see physical violence as an evil rather than structural maladies.

The three films we have discussed are a neat typology of the three basic positions regarding violence. D. W. Griffith based *Birth of a Nation* on an unexamined assumption that accorded with his Southern upbringing, namely, that the North was an unjust aggressor in promoting the abolition of slavery. We said that conservative-minded people are not quick to recognize institutional violence. That is true—*unless* they consider themselves victims of the drastic changes that law may bring about.

As for Sergei Eisenstein, his early films revealed an enthusiastic support of revolutionary Bolshevik ideas.[6] Like a matching book-end, *Potemkin* is a perfect counterpart to *Birth of a Nation*, not only as a cinema masterpiece but also to show that violence can be hallowed in the cause of the "have-nots." Someday perhaps we may see the critical discipline of the sociology of knowledge applied to motion pictures, especially to those *auteur* directors such as Griffith and Eisenstein who leave an indelible signature on their films. Both men are classic examples of Mannheim's distinction between ideology and utopia and the contrasting views of violence as a legitimate means to an end. In the case of Griffith, the end of the *status quo ante bellum*; in the case of Eisenstein it was revolutionary upheaval.

Medium Cool stands in the middle between ideology

and utopia, between the biases of Griffith and those of Eisenstein. This should not surprise us since the film is a documentary that aims principally at a stenographic chronicle of reality as depicted by the newsreel camera at the 1968 Chicago Democratic Nominating Convention. *Medium Cool* studies the interface of both extreme views of society and violence as they impinge on each other. Behind all violent encounters are ideologies, points of departure, unexamined assumptions, or what Eric Hoffer has called the attitude of "the true believer." Not only were Griffith and Eisenstein "true believers," as *Birth of a Nation* and *Potemkin* show, but so were Mayor Daley and the "yippies." Each disapproved of the form of violence they imputed to the other side and each felt eminently justified in using violence as a means of defense. Nowhere does "the Reel Revolution" make a greater contribution to a comprehensive understanding of liberation than in the examples it furnishes us regarding the forms and rationalizations underlying the use of violence.

NOTES

1. Cf. Hans Toch, *Violent Men: An Inquiry into the Psychology of Violence* (Chicago: Aldine Publishing Co., 1969).

2. Cf. Nevitt Sanford, Craig Comstock & Associates, *Sanctions for Evil* (San Francisco: Jossey-Bass, Inc., 1971).

3. Hugh Davis Graham and Ted R. Gurr, in their famous *Report to the National Commission on the Causes and Prevention of Violence*, observed that "Americans have always been given to a kind of historical amnesia that masks much of their turbulent past." See their *History of Violence in America* (New York: Praeger Publishing Co., 1970), p. xiv. Also see W. Eugene Hollon's *Frontier Violence: Another Look* (New York: Oxford University Press, 1974).

4. Cf. the report of Stanley Milgrim's experiments on "mandated violence" in *Human Relations*, 1965, 18 (1).

5. Bosley Crowther, "The Birth of a Nation," *The New York Times Magazine*, March 8, 1970; Robert M. Henderson, *D. W. Griffith* (New York: Oxford University Press, 1972).

6. Marie Seton, *S. M. Eisenstein* (London: The Bodley Head Press, 1952).

5.

The Anatomy of Exploitation

In his international best-seller, *The Wretched of the Earth*, the late Frantz Fanon gave a psychoanalytic view of the frustration and brimming resentment that millions of nonwhites feel toward the western colonializing powers. It has been only relatively recently that we have understood the nature of international stratification and the fact that there are poor classes and poor nations. In fact the poor within certain underdeveloped nations experience a double dependency—on the higher classes who rule the nation, which in turn depend on foreign investments and decisions abroad. This is the situation that characterizes the bulk of the world's poor. One of the directors who has dedicated himself to illustrating Frantz Fanon's thesis about the psychological imprinting of colonial peoples through decades and generations of dependency has been Gillo Pontecorvo, of France. In *The Battle of Algiers* (1966), he took the side of the Algerian liberationists against the French. We wish now to study the sequel to this film, *Burn!* in which Pontecorvo unmasks the decadence and eventual decline of social order that rests on colonial exploitation.

In all his films Pontecorvo casts one professional actor. In *Burn!* (1970), he casts Marlon Brando in the part of William Walker, an employee of the British company, Royal Sugar. The action takes place on a nineteenth-century Caribbean island, called Quemada (which means "Burnt"). Walker is commissioned to organize the natives so that Portuguese rule may be overthrown. As a step toward this objective he trains a powerful native dock worker, José Dolores (played by an illiterate Colombian peasant), and turns him into a rebel leader. Under Walker's tutelage and with British help Dolores leads a successful revolt, only to learn that the British prefer to install another as a puppet ruler. All that has happened is that the island of Quemada has changed rulers. Dolores is disappointed to find that he has been struggling for a pseudo-liberation movement and quickly mounts one that is more authentic. He becomes a guerrilla leader and overthrows the British. As the island's new ruler, he discovers that dependency has ended in one form but that, because of its mono-product economy, Quemada needs international markets for its sugar. Putting off his romantic revolutionary mantle, Dolores assiduously applies himself to understanding the dynamics of international trade and the complexities of supply and demand.

The British do not remain idle, especially as it becomes progressively apparent that the success of Quemada's revolution is infecting other islands and neighboring nations with the virus of national independence. Years have passed and William Walker, now knighted as Sir William Walker, returns with a mandate to overthrow Dolores and restore the island to British rule. As we meet Walker, we see an alcoholic, cynical servant of power who cannot help admiring José Dolores, the rebel leader whom he shaped as Pygmalion shaped Galatea in the classic Greek legend. The ambivalence of the relationships between oppressed and oppressor in such typical colonial circumstances is well captured in Pontecorvo's film. The colonizers want the loyalty and respect of those they control; the colonial peoples resent the foreign rule at the same time they realize that without the example and initial help of empire-builders they would never have taken the first step into modernization and western ideas of autonomy and dissent. One late scene shows the returning Sir William Walker on horseback in pursuit of the elusive José Dolores of whom Walker seems proud now that he has learned to be independent.

The vitality, integrity, and single-mindedness of José Dolores contrasts strikingly with the alienation and duplicity of Sir William Walker, played convincingly by Brando. Incidentally, it is revealing to compare the roles of the older Brando in *Burn!, The Godfather*, and *The Last Tango in Paris* with his early "tilted-pelvis" roles of defiance in *A Streetcar Named Desire, On the Waterfront*, and *The Wild One*. Walker, obviously a talented but amoral man who deteriorates with the years, is made by Pontecorvo to be the personification of the Marxist theory that the socio-economic heritage of western civilization has been largely based on the exploitation of pre-industrial lands in Asia, Africa, and Latin America. In returning to Quemada, Walker believes that the time is opportune to recover the island. This time he states his plan in broad philosophical language, saying: "Between one historical period and another, ten years may be enough to reveal the contradictions of a century." He is undoubtedly a master strategist and knows that the island cannot live from its own resources without trade contacts. Despite his secret admiration for Dolores, Walker assumes the attitude of a ruthless warlord, bent on burning every blade of grass on Quemada in order to defeat Dolores once and for all.

The mercenary Walker succeeds in capturing Dolores but is shrewd enough to see that he should not make a martyr of him. On the other hand, Dolores realizes that in his death will be born the hope of subsequent generations regarding liberation and self-determination. Dolores does die, only after taunting his captor with these words: "Civilization belongs to whites. But what civilization? Until when? " Pontecorvo has adopted a Marxist viewpoint in *Burn!*, showing how international interests, both political and economic, prevent the Third World from producing its own civilization. There is no Christian liberation viewpoint in *Burn!* It is a plea for direct political action, not through consciousness raising or democratic mechanisms of consensus engineering.

Pontecorvo missed an opportunity to penetrate psychologically into the character of Sir William Walker to show more subtly the personal ravages inflicted upon him as an instrument of foreign domination. It has been suggested that "Pontecorvo fears that moments of psychological insight in a film involve indulgence, a resort to what Marxists might call 'bourgeois individualism.' "[1] In any event, the rich resources of Brando's acting potential in this part were, unfortunately, not fully tapped.

Burn! is an important film contribution to understanding the liberation process. For one thing it shows that the "escape from" factor is easier to identify than the term of liberation, namely the prospective Promised Land. Karl Mannheim, as we have seen, distinguished between "absolute utopias" and "relative utopias." The latter refer to institutional changes that are attainable, whereas the former encompass all attempts to create ideal societies that are beyond any reasonable hope of achievement. Any science of the liberation process must call attention to the fact that revolutionaries of the ultra-left (such as José Dolores) deny that there is any such thing as absolute utopias. They affirm that all their liberation ideals are attainable—at least implicitly. On the other hand, the ideologues of the ultra-conservative right (such as Sir William Walker) tend to classify any movements for change, even those that are clearly incremental, as ideals of an absolute utopian nature.

That is why the process of liberation is fraught with so much danger, because emotion, vested interest, and passionate beliefs produce diametrically opposed views of the same situation. A science of liberation can help toward a diagnosis of the rights, the claims, and the responsibilities inherent in any conflict situation. Mutual misperception is inevitable where interests are opposed. The reciprocal spiral of distrust, fear, and hatred is clearly depicted in Pontecorvo's *Burn!* even though the director has a reasonable bias on behalf of the nonwhite colonial people symbolized by José Dolores.

Not only are there international situations of dependency; there is also internal colonialism within countries that pride themselves on being developed and democratic. A film masterpiece that serves admirably as a case study of the "underdog" within the United States is John Ford's screen version of John Steinbeck's best-selling novel, *The Grapes of Wrath* (1940). The film is faithful in capturing the biblical aura of the book and its theme of persecution, exile, and promise of deliverance. The movie boasts an outstanding cast—Henry Fonda as Tom Joad, Jane Darwell as Ma Joad, and John Carradine as the preacher. The Joads are a farm family in "dust bowl" Oklahoma during the worst depression years of the 1930s. Unable to meet the bank payments, they lose their farm and are compelled to pack their scanty possessions, load up their rickety truck, and begin the long exodus to what is for them the Promised Land of California. There they hope to find work as pickers in the groves of the large fruit plantations.

The "Okies" is the name given to the migrant workers from Oklahoma. They are clearly victims of an exploitative system in which financial abstractions take priority over flesh-and-blood people who lack the intelligence or the coping skills to deal with such paper realities as mortgages, interest payments, and profit-and-loss statements. For decades after the appearance of Steinbeck's powerful social exposé, the lot of the U.S. migratory workers did not improve appreciably— mainly because of their inability to bring organized pressure to bear on their employers, on their local communities, or on their elected representatives. Cesar Chavez in the sixties changed this. His charismatic leadership helped to catalyze the discontent of families such as the Joads and to channel it into effective outlets of protest and countervailing power.

Steinbeck's book and Ford's movie were part of the consciousness-raising process of the 1930s. The movie version of *The Grapes of Wrath* is often seen on TV reruns and so still exercises enduring influence as an agent of social change; not to mention the new generations of young readers who discover the Steinbeck tale of the forced trek across seven states, the subhuman living conditions, the indifference of public agencies, the calloused abuse of human rights by the fruit growers, and the futility of strikes due to lack of public support outside the subculture for the migrant workers themselves. In a sense, *The Grapes of Wrath*, like *Burn!*, showed a situation where violence was the only alternative. José Dolores and Tom Joad chose violence—reluctantly, to be sure, but still they chose it. Moreover they were both symbols for others. If Cuba or Quemada had been a state of the union of the United States, no structural changes would have occurred, for any attempt to change the system is seen as subversive. What happened in Cuba through force and was happening in Chile under Allende is inimical to U.S. theories of change. *The Grapes of Wrath* is a social protest in the best U.S. "muck-raking" tradition, whose nonrevolutionary axiom seems to be: "Bacteria cannot live in sunlight!" In the United States change is supposed to come about through consciousness-raising and legislation, not a change of the economic substratum.

Our last film study of exploitation is one that brings us closer to the contemporary period with its military take-overs and repressive governments. The French director Costa Gavras carved a niche for himself in the cinematographic Hall of Fame by his picture *Z* (1970). The letter Z in Greek is a symbol of hope—"He lives!" The reference is to the democratic socialism that was snuffed out by the military coup of the Greek colonels in April 1967. All democratic forms of protest were suppressed in the name of "anti-Communism"; thousands of persons were taken prisoners by the military government. The movie brings out clearly how moderate voices for change can be misperceived as a threat to those who stand to lose by any change. Once again the distinction between "absolute utopias" and "relative utopias" is crucial for understanding the deeper meanings of this masterly film.

The star of the film is Yves Montand, who plays Lambrakis, a very popular deputy of the Greek Congress and a candidate for the presidency. His wife is played by Irene Papas. At a rally, Lambrakis is assassinated. We learn that the killing was contracted by fascist elements of the armed forces aided by the police and high officials of the legal system. There is no clear allusion to conservative civilian supporters among the professional, merchant, and industrial groups, but we can reasonably assume that these constituted the main client group for the chief architects of the crime. The subsequent drama consists in a race between those who want to cover up the crime by silencing witnesses and publicists and those who are intent on getting the full facts in the political murder case. Jean-Louis Trintignant plays a crusading attorney for the state who indicts several of the Greek colonels after he gathers conclusive evidence of their participation in the death of Lambrakis. Suddenly, however, democracy has its last breath crushed out in the vise of the military coup. Political prisoners are rounded up. Persons who earlier were merely dissenters for a legitimate democratic cause now are branded as enemies of the state. The film ends on a brilliant note—listing all those who disappeared or committed suicide or were sentenced by martial law. Among these appears the name of the courageous prosecuting attorney (Trintignant).

Costa Gavras's *Z* not only presents the anatomy of exploitation in a historical moment of modern Greek history; it is the story in essence of every campaign of terror and military intervention to prevent change. Some have drawn an analogy between *Z* and the events following the election of Salvador Allende as the president of Chile. There were savage campaigns against Allende before his election and systematic attempts to prevent him from taking office. Whatever the criticisms of Allende's government or person, he began and terminated his rule as a president legitimately installed in power by the people. Over 35 percent of the voters, those who elected him and supported him through successive constitutional crises, were arbitrarily declared enemies of the state and, at the very least, came under the shadow of suspicion.

It is interesting that during Allende's presidency Costa Gavras went to Chile to film *State of Siege*, a movie that also dramatically analyzed exploitation, focusing in this case on Uruguay's Tupamaros and the killing of a U.S. AID official. Costa Gavras seems to have abandoned in *State of Siege* the hope he signalled at the end of *Z*. It is as if he sees the reciprocal spiral of violence as a constant of the human condition. In *State of Siege*, Costa Gavras utters a curse on the "change-seeking" left and the "change-shy" right, both, to his mind, equally inclined toward mindless violence. Films about polarized situations in Africa include historically based incidents in Algiers *(Battle of Algiers)*, Egypt *(Khartoum)*, Tunisia *(Ramparts of Clay)*, South Africa *(Zulu)*, and Kenya *(Something of Value)*. Exploitation and social cleavages reveal unique characteristics in Africa as contrasted with Europe, North and South America, and Asia.

We have examined three films dealing with exploitation; each has given us a different perspective on the problem. *Burn!* is an unusual film within the genre of commercial entertainment features: It confronts squarely the problem of colonialism and imperialism, daring to criticize the very countries that would serve as the principal markets for the motion picture. Shock, as Eisenstein knew, is often a function of class values. Middle-class audiences were not the patrons of *Burn!* As is often the case in media, those who go to hear or see an experience do so to reinforce their already existing beliefs. The counterculture and radical political adherents sought out *Burn!*

What is often not appreciated by those for whom films like *Burn!* seem extreme is that the Marxist diagnosis is not the same as the Marxist proposals for a better society. The class-struggle thesis of Marx often finds valid-ity in Third World countries—not only within nations but also in terms of relationships between developed and developing countries. The story of the Caribbean island Quemada supports the Marxist diagnosis and so is a factor that must enter into a science of liberation.

Marxists have success in areas such as Quemada precisely because of their ability to predict the behavior of the ruling classes and foreign interest groups. There is an old Roman adage that says that it is no disgrace to learn from an adversary *(Fas est doceri ab hoste)*. In the United States, Marxism is definitely a negatively charged word, yet Marxism has put a science of liberation into its debt because of its stress on the influence, often subconscious, of economic factors in distorting perception and thus helping to shape "false-consciousness."[2] We must learn to recognize the William Walkers not only on the screen but in real life as well. More important for their own personal liberation is the need for these same William Walkers to recognize themselves.

The Grapes of Wrath is also valuable in helping us form the habit of recognizing both who we are and what the structures we support are. Migratory workers are part of that invisible America about which Michael Harrington wrote so eloquently in his well-known book, *The Other America*. In every society there is "dirty work" to be done—work which is essential and yet which those who are comfortable want kept out of sight. Social justice movies are not among the big box-office successes, as a rule. Although *The Grapes of Wrath* captured the attention of the world, both as a novel and as a Hollywood film, it will never enjoy the success of *The Godfather* or *The Exorcist*. The perpetration of evil in dramatic forms has always been more alluring than the plight of the poor.

Why did *Z* succeed as a film which opened the curtain on the headline events of a national military coup by reactionary forces? The movie scenario, adapted from Vassili Vassilikos's book, took us into the secret pathways of power. This is always intriguing. Murder, courtroom drama, suspense, automobile chases, and chicanery supplied elements that make for movie success. *Z* did not show us the plight of those who would have benefited from the rule of Lambrakis, had he lived and been elected. The anatomy of exploitation was confined to the upper power levels and the villains were as easily identifiable as in *The Godfather*.

Al Pacino's role in *The Godfather II* paralleled that of Welles in *Citizen Kane*—power gone unchecked with tragic family consequences. In any scientific approach to liberation we must steel ourselves to look not only at what is dramatic and easily condemnable but also at what pricks us and reveals to us not what we think we are but what we are. Man's inhumaneness is a commonplace truth. But our inhumanity to others through the cultures, institutions, and structures we support is less difficult to accept. *Burn!*, *The Grapes of Wrath*, and *Z* are important contributions of "the Reel Revolution" toward a science of liberation and, I hope, our own personal liberation and full human development.

The Italian cinema in the past decade has dealt with the chemistry of exploitation in the Fascist period. Evocations of the period can be found in several distinguished Italian films of the seventies: Fellini's *Amarcord*, Bernardo Bertolucci's *The Conformist* and *The Spider's Stratagem*, and Lina Wertmuller's *Love and Anarchy* and *Seven Beauties*. For example, *Seven Beauties* opens with a stunning montage of Il Duce, Hitler, and scenes of battlefield carnage and aerial bombings. The role of private groups such as industrialists and the church within Nazi Germany is seen in Luchino Visconti's *The Damned* (1970) and Otto Preminger's *The Cardinal* (1963). Soviet slave camps are treated in films based on works by Alexander Solzhenitsyn: *The First Circle* and *One Day in the Life of Ivan Denisovich*. In this motion picture, important political prisoners, such as uncooperative scientists and engineers, were consigned to the hellish "first circle" camp to work on secret projects for the state that branded them traitors.

In U.S. society, exploitation tends to be more indirect than dramatically oppressive as in totalitarian states. However, there is pungent social commentary in such U.S. films of the seventies as *Save the Tiger* (Jack Lemmon is a harassed clothing executive at the mercy of grasping, amoral buyers), *Shampoo* (Warren Beatty is the Beverly Hills hairdresser with no moral substance or career direction), *Dog Day Afternoon* (Al Pacino is an idiosyncratic gunman who reveals the absurdities of such institutions as banks, TV broadcasting, and the local and federal police), and *All the President's Men* (Robert Redford and Dustin Hoffman play Woodward and Bernstein, the reporters who exposed the Watergate fiasco). Sidney Lumet's *Network* exposed TV power.

Nor should we overlook films of this decade which deal with the not too subtle forms of female exploitation and the challenges that face urban U.S. women: Carrie Snodgrass's frustrated wife and mother in *Diary of a Mad Housewife*, Barbra Streisand's distraught West Side housewife in *Up the Sandbox*, Ellen Burstyn's widowed mother in search of a new identity in *Alice Doesn't Live Here Anymore*, and Gena Rowland's mad wife in *Woman Under the Influence*.[3] As oppressed as these women are, their range of options is considerably broader than, say, the choices available to the male protagonists in Lina Wertmuller's films.[4] Thus oppression is relative to cultures, climes, and creeds. Movies are a veritable encyclopedia of the exploitation of people by people. The old saying that people are wolves in their dealings with other people (*homo homini lupus*) is verified again and again in the film output of all nations. For example, Satyajit Ray's *Distant Thunder* looked at the man-made Bengal famine that in 1942 caused three million deaths. What violence economic gain can produce!

NOTES

1. Joan Mellen, "A Reassessment of Gillo Pontecorvo's BURN! " *Cinema*, Winter, 1972–73, pp. 39ff.

2. James Roy MacBean, *Film and Revolution* (Bloomington: Indiana University Press, 1975).

3. See Molly Haskell, *From Reverence to Rape* (New York: Holt, Rinehart & Winston, 1974); Joan Mellen, *Women and Their Sexuality in the New Film* (New York: Horizon Press, 1974); Marjorie Rosen, *Popcorn Venus: Women, Movies and the American Dream* (New York: Coward, McCann & Geoghan, 1974).

4. Judy Klemesrud, "Wertmuller: The Foremost Woman Director," *The New York Times*, Arts & Leisure, February 9, 1975.

6.

The Liberation Philosophy
of Chaplin

No one has so dominated the motion picture industry
as Charlie Chaplin. Not using language, Chaplin made
his contemporary world and all subsequent generations
familiar with the "little tramp," and through him has
made towering contributions to a film primer on the
science of liberation.

Chaplin was uniquely endowed to be an eloquent
spokesman for the oppressed and the poor. He was born
in the poverty-stricken Kensington district of London in
1889 and learned to eat of the bitter fruit of deprivation
and hardship. He later confessed that no degree of affluence could ever efface the boyhood fears he had of the
impending hunger each new dawn brought. He once
said: "I am like a man who is ever haunted by a spirit,
the spirit of poverty, the spirit of privation."[1] Chaplin
became acquainted with a wide variety of types from the
milieu around him—one reminiscent of a Dickens novel.
Making his theatrical debut at six, the budding mimic
studied character: the tavern-keeper, the London
bobby, the blind violinist, the costermonger, the
wealthy matron, the exacting landlord, the prostitute,
and the drunkard. Everywhere were the "haves" and

the "have-nots." The young Chaplin smouldered with longings for social protest and artistic expression. The years with Dame Poverty would provide him with many lasting street impressions, thus helping him to evolve a repertoire of routines designed to meet customer approval in an eight-minute skit.[2]

Avoiding banalities and low comedy, Chaplin mastered situational poses, human reactions, and facial expressions to such a degree that he instinctively fulfilled Henri Bergson's belief that laughter appeals to pure intelligence. True, he employed sight gags and physical humor, but the pathos that Charlie evoked is essential to understanding why we laugh at his enemies and with his triumphant stratagems. In this sense, all of Chaplin's films have a dimension of conscientization that can be brought to the surface by critical reflection. The character of Charlie is, at bottom, a living "anti-project." Whereas Capra's heroes in *Mr. Deeds Goes to Town*, *Mr. Smith Goes to Washington*, and *Meet John Doe* are popular reformers, Chaplin is the eternal "nay-sayer." He symbolized the person on the margin of society, the person society needed but always overlooked, the "underdog," the *déraciné*.

Through the garb of the comic tramp, Chaplin satirized the effete social world of pre-World War I London: the undersized derby, the shoes with upturned toes, the cane, the cravat, and the rose in the lapel. Like a child pricking a toy balloon, Charlie deflated the pretensions of the reasonable world around him, especially where it seemed so secure, namely in its pride and symbols of status. The art of Chaplin cannot be divorced from his social gospel. Even later when Chaplin steps out of the character of the lovable tramp we see this social indignation at work as the orator calling the democracies to unite at the end of *The Great Dictator*, or as the Bluebeard killer of parasitic women in *Monsieur Verdoux* or as the critic of America's consumer, anti-Communist society in *A King in New York*.

Millions of "little people" identified with him, and his comic genius made the wealthy and pompous oblivious that he was "putting them on." He would extract a butt from a sardine can with all the grace of a millionaire opening his gilt cigarette case. Pretty girls tend to reject Charlie *(The Gold Rush* and *Modern Times* are exceptions); policemen pursue him; polite society scorns him. Whatever he undertakes invariably fails. He tries to enter a subway only to be carried helplessly along in the opposite direction by the crowd. He tries to open a Murphy bed only to be imprisoned in it. Even nature offers puckish resistance: The water hose drenches him and the wind carries away the melody he plays while serenading a pretty girl.

Why did the "little people" around the world identify with Charlie? Because he was a symbol of hope. He was a utopian character, utterly detached and always clinging to his personal dignity despite adverse events and society's misperception of his intrinsic worth. Some have seen in Charlie a type of wandering Jew, condemned to travel from place to place, ever shrugging his shoulders and starting down a road without horizons to pursue some new dream of happiness, of hope.[3]

Chaplin never lost sight of contemporary events and the moods of his audiences. He was very much immersed in history, and the socio-economic vicissitudes of the changing times always colored his message. The strike in *Modern Times* resembles the revolutionary moment in Eisenstein's *Strike*. The generations of the World War I period felt the discipline of conscription and the urgency of military defense. Chaplin produced *Shoulder Arms*, in which he played a buck private, an incarnation of Tommy Atkins or a latter day Private Hargrove. For millions of movie-goers, Charlie was the human cipher in the complex military bureaucracy. When mail comes, his gleeful anticipations melt to sharp disappointment as he finds out that there is no mail for him. However, he sees a comrade reading a letter and peers over his shoulder to read it, thus sharing the joy of the other. There is a liberating note, a simplicity and freedom from self-pity and resentment, that revolutionaries and ideologues do not always reflect in their attitudes. In such scenes Charlie taught his audience the lesson of human character and how a magnanimous soul confronts disappointment. The earlier Charlie of the Mack Sennett days was impish, even vindictive and malevolent. However he evolved and his character mellowed: The films of the twenties reveal a lovable Charlie who has no resentment. In a famous scene in *Modern Times* we see the prankster, Charlie, defusing the solemn atmosphere of the assembly-line factory. No one has symbolically resisted the depersonalization process more successfully than Chaplin. Humor, indeed, is the stamp of humanity. Revolutionaries can easily forget this.

In the "roaring twenties," with the appearance of the nouveaux riches and giddy levels of prosperity, Chaplin made comic masterpieces that showed how humanity could flourish despite social inequality. In *The Vagabond*, *The Circus*, *The Kid*, and *The Gold Rush*, Chaplin showed that independence came at a great personal price: loneliness.[4] His films were in sharp contrast to the average Hollywood film of the twenties, which capitalized on adventure, eroticism, rural sentimentality, urban alienation, slapstick humor, and the horror of the Lon Chaney movies. People laughed at a film such as *The Circus* but went away with the melancholy conviction that gaiety could mask sadness and that crowds harbored many lonely people. It is interesting that whenever Charlie is attracted to a companion, it is someone who is a social outcast—the street urchin in *The Kid*, the blind flower girl in *City Lights*, the homeless girl in *Modern Times*, the suicide-prone ballerina in *Limelight*. Audiences were attracted to this Charlie who knew that to lose at one level is to gain at another. Less can be more.

The generation of the thirties felt the pinch of worldwide depression. Chaplin responded with *City Lights* and *Modern Times*, two films that showed the drama of the individual pitted against economic deprivation and the industrial machine. When totalitarianism and fascism made headlines in Hitler's Germany and Mussolini's Italy, Chaplin countered with *The Great Dictator* and later, in the age of the nuclear bomb, with *Monsieur Verdoux*, the most negative film Chaplin ever made. In it Chaplin plays a man forced out of work by an acquisitive and unfeeling social order; he decides to support his family by marrying and successively murdering a number of rich widows. Perceptive critics have seen in *Monsieur Verdoux* the little tramp come back in disguise to wreak revenge on those flighty women who would not have him, to take by violence what society in its calloused indifference had denied him, and to fight hypocrisy and cunning with its own arms.

Some of the lines have a haunting wisdom. After receiving the death sentence, Verdoux calmly addresses the court: "I shall see you all very soon." He defends himself in a court of higher justice, saying: "One murder makes a villain; millions a hero." To the priest who visits him on the day of his execution, he remarks: "I am at peace with God, my conflict is with man." The pathetic fatalism is gone, so is the hope of the long winding road. In the final scene, this transfigured Charlie (now a Bluebeard) begins a stark lonely march to death. What a dramatic contrast to the last scene in *Modern Times*, where Charlie, hand-in-hand with Paulette Godard, turns his back on mass-production society to disappear down the unending road leading into a utopian future. *Monsieur Verdoux* hints at the same lessons found in so many of the future-oriented films: that people are prisoners of their own illusions and their own exaggerated trust in technology and social conventions. In effect, people work toward negative utopias under the false sign of progress and affluence.

Monsieur Verdoux must be seen within the total context of Chaplin's earlier films. The "little tramp" always seemed to find a door, an escape hatch in the confining walls of industrial society. Nothing was farther from Charlie's philosophy than nihilism. In Chaplin's films, there were echoes of the Old Testament liberation theme: The weak are delivered providentially from the strong. The celluloid puppet that he created in Charlie the tramp always triumphed in the face of the greatest odds. Even his lack of speech added to his weakness and, in an ironic way, provided him with greater powers of self-expression. There is an unquestionable David-Goliath motif in the Chaplin films of the silent era (down to and including *City Lights*). Despite his frail physique, he triumphs consistently over the obese employer, the powerful policeman, the bully, the brawny gangster, and the buxom matron. He is a symbol of the spirit opposing matter, the ethereal versus the corporeal. Consider the film *Easy Street*. Out of love for a minister's daughter, Charlie becomes a policeman. Not only does he succeed in subduing the powerful lawbreaker by partially asphyxiating him with a gasburner, but he brings him to honesty. Not only does David triumph over Goliath; instead of killing him he converts him. This is the technique of Mahatma Gandhi,

Martin Luther King, Jr., and Paulo Freire as discussed elsewhere: overcoming the oppressor without becoming an oppressor in turn.

Liberation is a process with no easy stages of growth and progress. It involves a tension between acceding to the will of the oppressor and resisting with force. Liberation is basically a spiritual force that seeks to unhinge the causes of oppression and injustice in both the victim and the exploiter. It is this dilemma that Chaplin faced squarely in the films that featured the "little tramp." *The Pilgrim* is an extraordinary filmic experience in the study of the "David-Goliath" motif and prophetic denunciation. Charlie is a fugitive from prison. He is taken for a minister and through force of circumstance finds himself in the pulpit, where he delivers in pantomime a moving sermon about the battle of David with Goliath. A small child applauds and typically Chaplin takes bows as if he were on the stage of a theater. The congregation is touched by this silent eloquence which is so much more profound than the conforming rhetoric of the better trained but hypocritical minister. When Charlie is finally found out to be an imposter he is pursued by the police. He crosses the Mexican border only to meet an oncoming band of hostile bandits. He races back to the border and there sees the approaching law officials. The audience sympathizes keenly with Charlie's plight. He has never been seen more marginal: caught between two pincer movements, one the official voice of "law and order" and the other the symbol of violent dissent to society's conventions. The film ends with Charlie straddling the border with one foot in the U.S.A. and the other in Mexico, running along the boundary line.

Charlie is not a confrontationist, not a guerrilla, not a collaborationist. He does not want to work for some future utopia that he himself cannot enjoy. He is an "im-

mediatist," that is, he takes the cash of personal freedom and lets pass the credit of social betterment, generally a future reward for others. Charlie always managed
to escape the social restrictions, many arbitrary, that
civilized life—so sensitive to property, status, profits,
and security—raises against those who are disenfranchised. Escaping by going over, under, around, or
through the obstacles placed by society, Charlie invites
the audience to follow him into the rosy dawn of tomorrow. One could see in this a certain nihilism or an op-
portunism characteristic of the streetwise marginal
person: the London cockney, the Mexican *pelado*
(Cantinflas), the Chilean *roto*, the New York hipster, the
Indian rickshaw wallah. But let us never forget that the
poor have few options and hope is their greatest re-
source.

The truth is that Chaplin's Charlie—known interna-
tionally by different names such as Charlot, Carlino,
Carlos, Carlitos, Kärlchen—is a one-man "liberation
process." He does not point to liberation; he symbolizes
it. However there is a cost: He is a "victim"—one who
knows that he is. Take the close-up of *City Lights* (1931),
that eloquent farewell to the silent movie. The flower
girl, her sight restored, discovers through her sensitive
sense of touch that the miserable tramp before her is the
benefactor whom she was led to believe was a millionaire. As we see the enlarged face of Charlie, it distills all
the shame and embarrassment of one who has fallen
from social status. Charlie's tramp was a witness, a
poignant mute witness to the inconsiderateness of society. In the silent period of Chaplin (1914–32), the "little
tramp" never took himself or society very seriously. And
yet he revealed himself as a highly sensitive creature
whose wounded feelings are capable of evoking great
pity. Amid the distress of being rejected, Charlie bore
life's bruises with great dignity, that dignity of the

"common person" which surpasses wealth, prestige, collectivism, and industrial efficiency.

In *City Lights* we have a classic instance of how he could detonate with laughter the somber but frail structures of a highly stratified society. When he swallows a whistle and enters a fashionable salon, he de-mystifies the atmosphere with every breath, producing a hilarious involuntary whistle. This is a "utopian" scene, suggesting a better social arrangement in which people would be more spontaneous and not labelled by the expectations of the powerful or the more educated. With boundless recuperative powers, Charlie meets every setback, especially those arbitrary, often capricious, rules of etiquette, by which society seeks to cabin and confine the unpredictable nature of the powerless.

Chaplin has been a stormy petrel in the United States. After *The Great Dictator* (1939), Chaplin began to run into unpopularity due to unfavorable publicity regarding his private life and his unconcealed criticism of the American way of life. Chaplin refused to become a naturalized citizen despite thirty years of residence in the U.S. The final estrangement of Chaplin from the United States occurred in 1947 when the State Department refused his re-entry permit when he visited London for the premiere of *Monsieur Verdoux*. After the pessimism of this film, Chaplin did *Limelight* (1952), which was an apt vehicle for his many-sided genius as writer, producer, director, music composer, actor, and discoverer of talent. With Claire Bloom, Chaplin enacted a modern parable of resurrection. A disillusioned dancer, Terry, attempts suicide and is saved by an aging vaudevillian, Calvero. They support one another. Calvero finds renewed purpose in life, while Terry regains confidence in her talent and in the possibility of happiness. The movie ends when Calvero slaps Terry during the intermission of her important debut as a ballerina and forces her to go on. At that moment he has an attack and dies. While he is carried off, she is seen pirouetting on stage. She is renewed in Calvero's death just as Charlie, the lovable tramp, is reborn in Verdoux's death. As Terry glides out onto the stage, Calvero utters a prayer to the Unknown God. This is a message of hope and renewal—a new dimension in Chaplin's theme of personal liberation.

Chaplin attempted in *A King in New York* (1957) an ambitious but unsuccessful exposé of anti-Communism in the United States, with its dependence on advertising, materialism, and an escalating standard of living. An exiled king of Estrovia finds popularity in the U.S. but is stigmatized because of his friendship with a small boy who has been investigated by Congress for his Marxist leanings. Once again Chaplin makes society the villain of his story as he portrays the persecution that besets the nonconformist. In *A King in New York*, Chaplin dons the mantle of a prophet, some latter-day Jeremiah, who calls society—in this case consumer-oriented capitalistic society—to repentance.[5] The film is too didactic and surrenders its artistic birthright for a pot of social message. But it is interesting as a comment by a supreme artist. Chaplin's credo was like that of another twentieth-century dissenter, James Joyce, who also chose exile in Switzerland. In *A Portrait of the Artist as a Young Man*, Joyce said, "I will try to express myself in some mode of life or art as freely as I can and as wholly as I can, using for my defence the only arms that I allow myself to use, silence, exile, and cunning."

A child of poverty, Chaplin has had a prophetic sense of mission. No other single person has so utilized the power of the screen to impress art, education, and entertainment into the service of liberation. We still have to catch up with the full implications of Chaplin's message. Whether or not Chaplin has Jewish ancestry (he has affirmed *and* denied this), there are certainly echoes of the "wandering Jew" theme in his films where Charlie surrenders everything but his dignity and freedom, the badges of his identity. There are frequent elements of the David-Goliath theme as we have already seen. There is a strong prophetic, even denunciatory, strain in Chaplin's films. In his anti-totalitarian film, *The Great Dictator*, Chaplin puts down his dramatic mask at the end of the film to face the audience and warn them explicitly of the dangers of dictatorial rule. There is also an exhilarating pastoral, even a Franciscan lyricism in the best Chaplin movies, in which the comic vagrant, freed from all material moorings, drifts effortlessly through life's troubled waters with a deep trust in that Providence that Shakespeare's Hamlet claims always "shapes our ends rough-hew them how we will." Chaplin has been knighted—he is now Sir Charles Chaplin—an ironic, though deserved, finale for the creator of the beloved "little tramp."

If we compare Chaplin with the great silent clowns, Buster Keaton, Harry Langdon, and Harold Lloyd, we will understand the greatness of Chaplin's "tramp" persona, not only as a remarkable artistic accomplishment but even as a paradigm for coping with social injustice. Chaplin is a guru whose transparency serves as a mirror: The dirt is on society's face, not on that of the "little tramp." This is not true of the Keaton who is a psychological study with virtually no oblique social commentary. As for Langdon, he was an adult-child who grew progressively infantile to the point of making the audience ill at ease. Lloyd's superactive persona was that of a pragmatic who could cope effectively with any and all situations—a sort of mute Bugs Bunny with confidence in his final victory. This assurance is absent in Chaplin, for whom the struggle and the pain are very real.

Chaplin is the patron saint of "the road." In being alone with him, we feel something archaic, something fundamental; we are not alone, we feel free. Chaplin is not anti-social nor a-social; he unites sociability with privacy. It is interesting to contrast the fulfillment that we the audience share with Chaplin as contrasted with the loneliness of the voyagers in the films of the late sixties and the seventies: *Chastity* with Cher as a hitch-hiker; *Five Easy Pieces* with Jack Nicholson as the rest-less piano-playing oilrigger; *Scarecrow* with Al Pacino and Gene Hackman as tragicomic "road-buddies"; *Harry and Tonto* with Art Carney in his Oscar-winning role as the wise itinerant retiree who receives more affection from his cat than from his three grown chil-dren; and *Payday* with Rip Torn as the "on-the-road" country-and-western singer who tours the South in his Cadillac. How sad the new "road" films are compared to the glorious silent comedies of Chaplin can best be judged from one review of *Payday*: "The American road is not open any longer: it has all been parcelled out and franchised off by Holiday Inns and McDonalds, Howard Johnsons and Colonel Sanders, national oil companies and state highway departments."[6] Chaplin walked slowly down the open road and tasted his liberty; con-temporary movie protagonists race down interstate highways and urban freeways on motorcycles, in cars, or as passengers in Greyhound buses.

No film study of the liberation process would be com-plete without considering the canon of Chaplin's films. Even today, younger generations watch him with open mouths, awed by his genius. And the poor still enjoy his appreciation of their joys, their disappointments, their humiliations. The eternal pilgrim, Chaplin's journey down the open road is a call to utopian thinking, to letting fall all those things we cherish and mistakenly think we cannot live without.[7] His territory flies no flag; it is an inner world sustained by remarkable resources of the spirit. It is a one-man crusade on behalf of human-kind, a compassionate examination of conscience regarding the person and society, poverty and wealth, law and equity, and freedom versus the trammels of institutions and rules. Chaplin has not only pushed cinematic art to exalted heights but has also given lasting witness—retrievable on celluloid for future generations—to the utopian nature of human beings. His legacy of films keeps bright the hope of a social order in which the individual, especially the more powerless, will not be effaced by wealth, social status, mechanization, dictatorship, or a specious form of democracy that serves the privileged rather than the majority.

Charlie, the "little tramp," has been for those leading lives of quiet desperation a "pillar of fire"—whether in the darkness of the subculture of poverty and underde-velopment or of a consumeristic society with compulsive technological rhythms of life. For Chaplin liberation is not verbal; it is not preachment. It means activating alternatives and giving witness by lifestyle. If seeing is revolutionary, as psychologists of art believe, then Chaplin qualifies as the complete revolutionary, forcing us to see through the veils and fictions of the social order to a deeper level of humanity. He must be considered quintessential to the process we are studying. He is par excellence "the Reel Revolutionary," even though he led no collective movement.

NOTES

1. Cited in René Jeanne and Charles Ford, *Histoire du cinéma américain*, vol. 3 of *Histoire Encyclopédique du Cinéma*, 1845–1945 (Paris: Robert LaFont, 1954), p. 248.

2. See my article "The Social Philosophy of Charlie Chaplin," *Studies*, Autumn 1960, pp. 313–20.

3. See Maurice Pontet, "La signification humaine de l'oeuvre de Charlie Chaplin," *Etudes* 282 (September 1954), p. 254; also Jean d'Yvoire, "La Ruée vers l'Or," *Téléciné*, June 1956, p. 5.

4. For an excellent treatment of these vintage Chaplin films, see Walter Kerr's *The Silent Clowns* (New York: Alfred A. Knopf, 1975).

5. Paul Lee, "Whither Chaplin?" *America*, October 5, 1957, pp. 12–14.

6. Russell E. Murphy, "Reviews: Payday," *Film Quarterly*, Winter 1973–74, pp. 47–49.

7. For a study of the pilgrimage motif in motion pictures, see Ernest Ferlita and John May, *Film Odyssey* (Paramus, N.J.: The Paulist Press, 1976).

8. Cf. Alexandre Arnoux, "Charlie Chaplin et le Cirque," *Du Muet au Parlant* (Paris: La Nouvelle Edition, 1946), pp. 35ff.

7.

Latin American Cinema
and Human Liberation

Though the number of Hispanic people, whether residents or citizens, is on the increase in the United States, most non-Hispanics still do not understand the culture, history, or character of the people. The winds of liberation first began to blow in Latin America in this century with the Mexican Revolution of 1910. A few years later occurred the Irish Rebellion and the Russian Revolution, events which are more publicized and better understood by Americans than the earlier Mexican movement of social justice for peasants, for Indians, and for the urban underprivileged. Latin American cinema is a blind area of interest even for critics. That is regrettable since fascinating themes appear in the movies produced in Argentina, Brazil, Chile, and Mexico.

The figure that stands out most clearly in Mexico's revolution is that of Pancho Villa, and after him the peasant rebel Emiliano Zapata. U.S. motion pictures have shown an abiding fascination with both figures. Wallace Beery played one of his most unforgettable roles in *Viva Villa!*, directed by Howard Hawks and Jack Conway, and Marlon Brando distinguished himself in the prime of his acting career as the protagonist in *Viva*

Zapata!, directed by Elia Kazan. After independence was gained from Spain in the nineteenth century, national movements of liberation sought to distribute power and opportunity in a more equitable way. The movement in Mexico took place as part of a revolutionary avalanche. Pancho Villa was active in the north of Mexico (Chihuahua); Zapata stirred up the peasants in the south (Morelos), while the less spectacular "landowner" revolutionary, Francisco Madero, operated in the more central region of Coahuila. The combined, if uncoordinated, movements of all three led to the overthrow of Porfirio Díaz, the first and perhaps best known of all the Latin American dictators (*caudillos*), who ruled Mexico from 1875 to 1911. The reader may be interested to know that the late John Garfield played the young Porfirio Díaz in one of Warner Brothers' more ornate productions, *Juarez*, in which Paul Muni starred as the renowned Indian-born liberator of Mexico, Benito Juárez. This historical epic is often shown on television.

One of the most disturbing Latin American films is a semi-documentary, *Camilo Torres* (1969), based on the life of the Colombian diocesan priest. Having studied sociology in Europe, Padre Torres returned to his homeland and served as Catholic chaplain at the National University in Bogota. As at many state universities in Latin America, Marxist influence prevailed (in contrast with private universities, which cater to students from upper-class origins). During his years as chaplain Torres became radicalized, especially as he became convinced that the role of the church was supportive of the status quo.

The film *Camilo Torres* does not develop the changing policy of the Catholic church under Pope John XXIII beginning with *Mater et Magistra* (1961) and continuing with *Pacem in Terris* (1963). The implication was that non-Catholics and even traditional rival groups such as Socialists and Communists could be potential allies (*Pacem in Terris*, Section 61). What the film does show, however, is the growing sense of futility that Torres experienced in conventional means of effecting social and political change. It also places Camilo Torres in a favorable light and harvests substantial sympathy for him when he dies as an armed guerrilla insurgent. Rebellion may repel many, but Luis Buñuel in *The Exterminating Angel* and *The Discreet Charm of the Bourgeoisie* shows that ruling elites are psychologically bound to the social structures of which they are virtual prisoners. They cannot change, Buñuel insists in his films. The corollary is the grinding misery of the ghetto poor, especially children, as in Buñuel's classic *Los Olvidados (The Young and the Damned)*.

The film we wish to discuss is a remarkable documentary, *Mexico: The Frozen Revolution* (1968), directed by Raymundo Glayzer. The film contains rare archival footage of the Mexican Revolution of 1910–17, as well as interviews with veterans of the revolution. It opens with violence and ends on the same note with the repression of the student uprising in 1968. Its purpose is to inform the spectator why the molten lava from the original volcano of the Mexican Revolution cooled down despite continual official protests to the contrary. The film shows the poverty of the peons, rural farmers who prefer to work the fewest possible hours in order not to enrich the estate-owners who usually are not interested in raising the standards of living of their peasant employees. In one scene we hear a tenant farmer express the lack of incentive for working any harder; in the next scene we hear a wealthy lady—owner of a profitable *hacienda*—describe how lazy the farmers are. The montage is worthy of Eisenstein and effectively reveals the sharp differences in the mental maps of the wealthy and the poor in Mexico's agricultural economy. The film also shows actual scenes from a campaign speech of Luis Echeverría.

The overall effect of the film is to show that behind the facade of the revolutionary democratic tradition initiated by Villa, Zapata, and Madero (all shot to death, incidentally) was an economic control group that used the revolution to serve their own particularistic aims.[1] The film's tragic irony spills over in the poignant scenes of the dead bodies of the hundreds of students who were massacred in their protest over the lamentable conditions of mass poverty, masked by the economic gains shared almost exclusively by the middle and upper classes.

Rafael Corkidi, a Buñuel devotee, directed a brilliant political allegory titled *Pafnucio Santo* (1976). The film hints that good and evil are intermingled in the Christian tradition, that a privatized spirituality has cloaked neglect of oppressive racial and social attitudes. Operatic arias highlight scenes in which a ten-year-old boy (Pafnucio Santo) is a type of angel-messenger searching for the ideal mother of a political messiah for Mexico. In the last scene we see a lithe, mustachioed revolutionary with broad-brimmed sombrero, crossed bandeleros, and pistols. He is a symbol for both Villa and Zapata, both shot in an open courtyard. As the revolutionary falls to the earth the next cut shows a pretty woman naked on the ground, but with crossed amnunition belts across her chest. Corkidi seems to be saying that she is the suitable mother of our "this-worldly" messiah. Clearly a secular socialist tract, *Pafnucio Santo* is a brilliant piece of revolutionary moviemaking (see the accompanying still photo). This film and *Mexico: The Frozen Revolution*

From Rafael Corkidi's Pafnucio Santo

capture the exciting promise of revolutionary change and the co-opting of the original spirit of justice and idealism to serve other, more elitist, purposes.

No treatment of Latin American films should overlook the famous comedian, Cantinflas (Mario Moreno), Mexico's salute to Charlie Chaplin. Cantinflas is the quintessential "born loser," the symbol for all Latin America's "forgotten people": the *pelados* in Mexico, the *rotos* in Chile, the *serranos* in Ecuador, the *cholos* in Peru. Cantinflas's self-conscious dignity has won for him millions of admirers in Latin America. Movies starring Cantinflas run for weeks and weeks; his fans, many from the lower classes, do not mind queueing up in long lines to buy their admission tickets. Anglo-Saxon and European film audiences, having seen Cantinflas only in cameo roles in films such as *Around the World in Eighty Days*, have no appreciation of his magnetic appeal to the underprivileged. Writing in the Chilean daily, *El Mercurio*, journalist Horacio Serrano has wittily observed of Cantinflas:

His contribution is his logic. . . . According to Aristotle, the Master, the conclusions in a syllogism are certain if the premises are true. But in Cantinflas's case, it is different. His conclusions are true only when the premises are not. Latin American politics, its history, and its economics are ruled by the logic of Cantinflas so that truth and imagination are mixed together in order to arrive at a deduction totally at odds with the starting point.[2]

Nordic people have difficulty understanding this logic that manages to imbue with spirit, humor, and authenticity the most oppressive, often fatalistic, circumstances.

An excellent example of this logic and its role in a study of liberation is the film *Your Excellency (Su Excelencia*, 1963). Cantinflas plays the part of a member of a delegation from a small "banana" republic to the

United Nations. In slapstick satirical style we see the portrait of the president of the country changed several times within the short span of time of a diplomatic banquet. When the final change of government leads to the appointment of Cantinflas as the official ambassador of his small nation to the U.N., the situation comedy has new possibilities added to it: the furious exchange of medals and gifts between Cantinflas and the ruler of a wealthy European nation; the rivalry between the two superpowers for the decisive vote on a crucial issue. The one power is called *Los Verdes* ("The Greens") and tries to win over Cantinflas, first through seduction by a beautiful spy who resembles Greta Garbo's Mata Hari and, when that fails, through threats on his life. The other power is called *Dolaronia* ("The Big Dollars") and tries to influence Cantinflas's vote by the promise of aid and investments. Beneath the admittedly grotesque caricatures of the Soviet Russia and the United States was a sentiment that was faithful to the way many Latin Americans from all social strata felt regarding their "in-between" position during the Cold War years of the fifties and sixties.

Your Excellency provided numerous laughs (for example, Cantinflas de-emphasizing the erotic overtures of the Russian spy by his inimitable dance routine as she tries to lower his resistance to her sexual allures). Nevertheless, in true Chaplinesque fashion, it made a profound point on behalf of the developing nations in the final, very moving scene. When he takes the podium to announce his country's vote in a plenary session of the General Assembly, Cantinflas becomes extremely solemn. He regrets that he cannot vote since he has resigned his post. Nevertheless he uses the occasion to deliver a very touching farewell address, reminding the distinguished audience that two thousand years earlier a simple carpenter taught that humankind should love each other and not engage in an arms race. (The original Spanish soundtrack contains a play on the words *amaos*, "love one another" and *armaos* "arm one another.") Silence falls on the assembled delegates as Cantinflas leaves the hall and tips the doorman by giving him a large medal from the lapel of his coat. He leaves as his secretary (also his girlfriend) takes his arm. Together they go down the path into the future in a scene reminiscent of Chaplin and Paulette Goddard at the end of *Modern Times*. *Your Excellency* is an excellent case of comedy in the service of consciousness-raising. Those in the middle and upper classes can often best be educated through humor.

The *cinema novo* of Brazil has offered a number of films: Ruy Guerra's *The Gods and the Dead, Os Fusis*, Nelson Pereira dos Santos's *Rio Quarenta Graus, Vidas Secas*. Instead of imitating Hollywood, as many Mexican films tended to do, Brazilian directors in the early and mid-sixties became aware of their obligation to use the medium of film to sharpen the self-awareness of their compatriots regarding the conditions in the steppes of interior Brazil (the *sertão*), the Matto Grosso, the fishing regions of Bahia, poverty-ridden Recife, the rapidly growing cities of São Paulo, Brasilia, and picturesque Rio de Janeiro. One of the best known exponents of *cinema novo* is Glauber Rocha. The reader can best sample his style through a familiarity with his masterly *Antonio das Mortes* (1969), a film that dramatizes the disorganization of the inhabitants of the remote and arid *sertão*, caught as they are in the web of superstition, ignorance, poverty, and corruption.

The chief figure is the military colonel, a total degenerate who reminds us of Brando's British imperialist in Pontecorvo's *Burn!* He is the symbol of feudal privilege. Not only the police but the clergy and the teachers are under his thumb. He pulls the wires so that all the agents of social control look to him for their cues. Coarse and empty, the colonel does not hide his dissolute life with his blonde mistress. Since his manipulation of the life of the region is direct and open, the inhabitants suffer a dual alienation—psychological as well as economic.

Often in *cinema novo*, as in *Antonio das Mortes*, religion and superstition are portrayed as mechanisms for release and supernatural hope, with no relevance to consciousness-raising or programs of structural change. *Antonio das Mortes* is a close, artistic examination of those "living dead" about whom Paulo Freire has written in assessing the hidden, more psychic costs of those whom privilege has corrupted and rendered callous. The photo on p. 117 conveys this sense of psychological asphyxiation, of ebbing hope. It deserves mention that the poorer sections of Brazil have not only inspired such world-famous directors as Glauber Rocha but also some of the most eloquent spokesmen on behalf of social justice: Archbishop Helder Camara, Paulo Freire, and Josue de Castro (author of *The Geography of Hunger*).

With the election of President Eduardo Frei in Chile in 1964 down through the government of Salvador Allende, Chilean movies reflected a deep concern for social change and national awareness. Films like *To Die a Little, The Long Journey*, and *The Jackal of Nahueltoro* showed the contrasts between rich and poor, the warped nature of children's lives in slum conditions, and the arbitrariness of official justice in the case of the disadvantaged. We wish to discuss a powerful Chilean film made and released during the Allende period, when the socialistic Popular Unity coalition exercised legitimate power. The film's title is *It Is Not Enough Just to Pray* (1971).

Overtly ideological in character, this film is a study of three Catholic priests in Chile during the period of revolutionary change that Allende and the Popular Unity coalition had initiated. Although the message of the film far outweighs its art, it does point up very neatly how men of the same faith and, indeed, even of the same sacerdotal vocation can differ on fundamental sociopolitical issues. As a resident in Chile during the period under discussion, the author can attest to the wide cleavages that existed within the Catholic hierarchy and clergy regarding the uncompromising socialist ideals of Allende's Popular Unity program. One of the priests portrayed is a parish curate in an upper-middle-class neighborhood (the "barrio alto") of Santiago. The movie depicts him as comfortable, indifferent to the plight of the masses, and firmly opposed to all but the most minor changes. In effect, he is a "sacristy priest," tending almost exclusively to the liturgical and sacramental life of his church and his congregation.

The second priest we meet is capable of identifying with the needs of the lower classes in Chile (at the time about one-third of the ten million inhabitants of the country). The consciousness of this priest needs no "raising"; he is fully *concientazado*. What he lacks, however, is an "anti-project," as Paulo Freire calls it; he has no way of committing his concern in terms of time, talent, and energy so that the situation of the poor can be ameliorated. This priest is a "reformist" rather than a revolutionary, but even his well-intentioned goals remain quite undefined—the product of "wish-fathered" thinking. Not only is this second priest not a leader, he seems unable to find a movement through which he can channel his obviously sincere and faith-inspired motives to serve a cause beyond that of his parish.

The third priest is not a revolutionary when we first

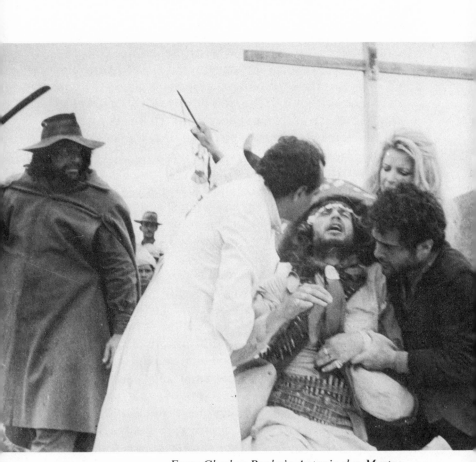

From Glauber Rocha's Antonio das Mortes

meet him, but becomes one in the final scene. This priest has had the same seminary training as the other two; his more radical position is traceable to his day-to-day contact with the condition of poverty. His is not merely a conceptual awareness of "white violence," that institutionalized form of pervasive injustice that closes off opportunity by having the needs of a society determined chiefly by purchasing power in the market system. One strongly suspects that the revolutionary priest, clearly the hero-type of the film, was modelled on Camilo Torres, the Colombian priest who, after serving as chaplain to students at the National University in Bogota, put down his cassock to become a guerrilla in the countryside. The federal troops finally shot Camilo Torres, thus making him a legendary martyr along with Che Guevara. (In sharp contrast to Hollywood's superficial film about *Che!*, the Latin American documentary about Camilo Torres is realistic and sympathetic.) In *It Is Not Enough Just to Pray*, the socially indignant priest picks up a rock to fling it in protest; the frame freezes as the film ends. Perhaps he too will go off as did Camilo Torres to become an armed militant, an avowed enemy of a bourgeois society. However, radical commitment need not embrace violence, as in the case of Camilo Torres.

Of the many revolutionary films made in Cuba since Castro's ascent to power, the first to be distributed in the United States e.g., *Memories of Underdevelopment* and *Lucia*, had difficulties being released here. Others, more entertaining, were very popular.

The Harder They Come (1969) features *reggae* music star Jimmy Cliff as Ivan, who comes out of the Jamaican hills to Kingston town with the dream of making it as a singer. He becomes involved in dope running. He does not trust the mob's authority and alienates them. Curiously, as with Peter Lorre's child-rapist in the classic *M*, he is hunted both by the mob and by the police (since he murdered a policeman).

For a brief time, Ivan experiences the exhilarating freedom that poverty-stricken youngsters yearn for. His record hits the top of the Kingston charts; he becomes a Robin-Hood type (writing graffiti such as "I am everywhere!"). His newspaper notoriety and elusiveness infuriate the police, who threaten to shut down the traffic in marijuana. His death is inevitable, but the audience feels no sense of tragedy; there is a sense of liberation that Ivan transcended the limits of the system. This film has run for years and has acquired a large cult following at the Elgin Theatre in New York City, where it is shown on weekends at midnight. "The prisoner thinks of only one thing—escape." The fans of *The Harder They Come* identify with the oppression from which Ivan manages to escape.

The French director Costa Gavras has distinguished himself with remarkable movies about contemporary political themes: the military takeover by right-wing Greek colonels in *Z*, the unscrupulous tactics of Communists in demanding unconditional allegiance to party discipline in *The Confession*, and the urban guerrilla movement in Latin America in *State of Siege*.

State of Siege (1972) is a cinematic synthesis of Costa Gavras's two earlier motion pictures, *Z* (1970) and *The Confession* (1971). The latter was an indictment of the abuses of Marxism in Eastern Europe; the former was an exposé of the ruthless nature of the military-capitalistic complex in Greece. In *State of Siege*, Costa Gavras pronounces a curse on both extremes simultaneously, using as a vehicle for his searing judgment the real-life study of the U.S. agent, Daniel Mitrione (a former Indiana police chief), who was murdered by the Uruguayan revolutionaries (the Tupamaros) after they had learned that Mitrione's assignment was to instruct law and order officials in Uruguay how to control through repression and even torture. Incidentally, a highly instructive if apologetic documentary was made to explain why the *Tupamaros* had recourse to limited violent acts such as kidnappings and massive prison breaks: Jan Lindquist's *Tupamaros*. This short film is a companion piece to *State of Siege*.

State of Siege was prohibited from being shown at the film festival that inaugurated the new theatre of the American Film Institute (AFI) at the John F. Kennedy Center in Washington, D.C. The AFI's director, George Stevens, Jr., complied with the request from the White House to withdraw the film on the grounds that it justified political assassination.[3] This occasioned a flood of criticisms to the effect that censorship was being exercised by President Nixon and his advisers in the White House.[4] This incident, in which political pressure prevented the premiere showing of *State of Siege* to a distinguished gathering in the U.S. capital, brings to mind a trenchant statement of Paulo Freire. In his incisive study *The Pedagogy of the Oppressed*, Freire points out that often the dominant class interprets efforts to seek full justice for all not as the humanization of society but as subversion of the existing order of things.[5]

What we miss in *State of Siege* is hope. Costa Gavras enables the spectator to see through the reciprocal nature of antagonistic blind commitment as it spirals into purposeless acts of reprisal and tactical "one-upmanship"—kidnappings, arrests, bombings, tortures, murder, and a general climate of fear and odium. *State of Siege* reflects the despair of Costa Gavras that any new type of human being will emerge from the human condition as we survey it dispassionately in the twentieth century. Many of the Brazilian *cinema novo* films end on a note of resignation, of fatalism. One is able to choose between going down and going down fighting.

The last film to be discussed is a highly controversial piece of "guerrilla filmmaking," *The Hour of the Furnaces* (1968)—unquestionably the boldest and most ambitious piece of moviemaking since the work of Sergei Eisenstein in the twenties.[6] The directors, Fernando Solanas and Octavio Getino, have been members of a group of revolutionary filmmakers in Argentina: El Grupo Ciné Liberación. *The Hour of the Furnaces* is part of Argentina's new wave, so different from the work of the world-renowned Argentinian director, Leopold Torre-Nilsson, who made a number of stylistic films about neo-Victorian family life in Buenos Aires and the ties between aristocratic wealth and trade union corruption in the Peron era. *The Hour of the Furnaces* subordinates film art to a revolutionary message, turning the camera into a machine gun that attacks the enemy's ideology by spewing forth a hail of activist ideas as if they were bullets.

In truly revolutionary fashion, *The Hour of the Furnaces* seeks to remove the spectator from any possible refuge in a neutral or uncommitted position that would, at bottom, serve the oppressive status quo that the directors condemn. Their film has as its premise the statement of Frantz Fanon: "Every spectator is either a coward or a traitor." Just as Fanon in *The Wretched of the Earth* describes the sequence of stages through which nations and groups must pass in order to achieve independence, so Solanas and Getino take their viewers through the same process by visually drawing them into the history of Argentina. The movie begins by accenting the effects of "white violence"—often hidden, even tolerated, by those who profit most from the institutional arrangement. We see underpaid workers, the abiding presence of armed police officials, alcoholism, aristo-

cratic vice, substandard housing, sickness, the lifestyle
of the rural oligarchy on their grand estates, the al-
liance between the industrial class and the military, the
inevitability of military takeovers as a way of prevent-
ing structural change and supporting the privileges of
the upper class. The film is as tendentious as Griffith's
Birth of a Nation and Eisenstein's *Potemkin*, without
attaining the level of artistic expression that those two
directors achieved. *The Hour of the Furnaces* is a radical
reinterpretation of recent Argentinian history, an excellent corrective for the official chronicles but over-
determined in its political direction.

In the second part of the film, the ideological goals of
the directors become clearer as they cultivate in the
audience a critical consciousness of what must be done.
The film records the period (1945–55) of Perón, his remarkable actress wife, Evita, and the enthusiastic, almost worshipful, loyalty that the working class and the
trade unions showed to them. The film follows Argentinian history through the period after Evita's death and
Perón's exile and covers the less-inspired leaders who
ruled, often as military dictators, during this period
(1955–66). This segment of *The Hour of the Furnaces*
does show the progress that was made despite obvious
shortcomings that directors Solanas and Getino highlight. Argentina did disentangle itself from foreign investments in the post–World War II period to achieve
greater independence—but far from a degree satisfac-
tory to the film's makers.

The third part of the film goes beyond the "anti-
project," that is, the critical awareness of Argentina's
slow progress toward liberation, and tries to teach the
spectator a revolutionary praxis. Genuine liberation
can never stop at awareness or at the level of rhetorical
appeals. Just as Fanon in *The Wretched of the Earth*
inculcated commitment to change, Solanas and Getino

immerse their audience in the process of historical exploitation in order to trigger a revolutionary response. This explains why the film is so lengthy (about five hours). Alternatives are suggested through scenes of activist groups and testimonies of socially-committed persons. The object is to make the viewer feel both personal as well as institutional guilt. A person may be an active member of an organization or system that denies others (e.g., minorities or women) their full rights and yet still be opposed to those policies by constituting with others a loyal opposition.

Perhaps this is the basic weakness of the film: It does not believe in loyal opposition, only violent revolution. The film coerces emotionally and does not leave the moviegoer free to respond in any other way other than that predesigned by the filmmakers. Their strategy is to induce a commitment to revolution by leading the viewer to see that those who are not part of the solution (understood as involvement in revolutionary praxis) are part of the problem (that is, an ally of the oppressors). The *Hour of the Furnaces* rules out reformist measures. Nevertheless it is a valuable film for the science of liberation, for it discounts the all-too-frequent comfortable "majoritarian" solutions that appear in our editorials, our round-table discussions, and our legislatures.

The movies made in Latin America and discussed in this chapter are an important contribution to a wider understanding of liberation.[7] It must be remembered that the United States was born modern, that is, without feudalism, and that Latin America accepted inequality as part of its Spanish heritage. In recent times, there has been an awareness among certain groups in Latin America that change is needed to democratize opportunities for the bulk of its people who have not been able to participate in the life of their countries.

U.S. films have not been as radical, mainly because of

the belief that conditions are not only better but improving in the United States. However, as U.S. cities become "black, brown, and broke," this assumption is less valid. Beneath the constitutional and traditional guarantees there is still much injustice and inequality. During the seventies, unemployment, hunger, and insecurity have grown, especially among the lower income groups and the minorities. It is conservatively estimated that 60 million Americans are "ill fed, ill clothed, and ill housed," almost the same ratio of a "third" about which Franklin D. Roosevelt spoke in his famous emergency address in 1933. We are not hearing a great deal about this submerged one-third of an affluent nation. The themes of the movies just discussed should be treated in the United States, but the films would run the risk of not being patronized. Martin Scorcese's remarkable *Mean Streets* failed at the box office partly because it presented a direct view of the underside of Italian immigrant life in New York City. I submit that many lessons to be learned from this chapter are just as relevant to the U.S. and Europe as to Latin America, Africa, or Asia. Let us briefly summarize what these are.

The Mexican Revolution, subject of both Hollywood and Latin American movies, proves what President John F. Kennedy once said, namely, that those who make peaceful change impossible make violent revolution inevitable. The cause of Pancho Villa and Emiliano Zapata was undeniably just. There are those who are swift to condemn the armed uprisings that have characterized independence movements in this century without being aware of the vast, often unseen, structures and relationships of oppression that we have termed "white violence." *Mexico: The Frozen Revolution* analyzes the gains made by the revolutionary legacy of Villa, Zapata, and Madero and shows that economic prosperity as measured by Gross National Product is not identical with social justice, since an elite can "cream off" the benefits of foreign aid, tourism, and socio-technological progress. *The Hour of the Furnaces* is a still more ambitious, Marxist-inspired, effort to show the same pattern of maldistributed opportunity and wealth in Argentina. These types of radical *cinéma vérité* films are unusual in the United States, where filmmakers prefer to unmask political processes, corruption, and wealthy celebrities (e.g., *Citizen Kane, Medium Cool, On the Waterfront, Face in the Crowd, All the King's Men, Advise and Consent, The Candidate*, and *The Godfather*, Parts I and II).

John Kenneth Galbraith made the perceptive observation in his book *American Capitalism: A Study in Countervailing Power* that power in the third person is always threatening, whereas power in the first person never is. The Mexican film, *Your Excellency*, starring Cantinflas, helps those who live in a nation considered a superpower to see how their home country looks to the less powerful nations. Here in the United States we are aware of foreign aid, the Peace Corps, and the sizeable investments made in Latin America, but little do we realize that over the decades the repatriation of dividends from those original capital outlays plus the immigration of "human capital" (nurses, doctors, engineers, and professional people trained in Latin America) have far outbalanced the aggregate benefits that the United States has bestowed on our neighbors to the South. *Your Excellency* only touched the surface of the problem of the less powerful nations vis-à-vis the superpowers.

It is no secret that the United States supported dictatorial regimes (Batista, Duvalier, Zamora, Stroessner) as the lesser of two evils in its fight against the spread of Marxism in the hemisphere. From the foreign policy viewpoint of our geopoliticians in the Pentagon, the State Department, and the Central Intelligence Agency, this may seem to be sound strategy, but in effect it can serve to buttress local authoritarian structures like those depicted in Glauber Rocha's *Antonio das Mortes*, Solanas and Getino's *The Hour of the Furnaces*, and Costa Gavras's *State of Siege*. Latin American movies make these associations, perhaps in an exaggerated way, but the corrective to our own neglect of those themes is salutary. In addition to the films mentioned here, we would also recommend *Campamento, Courage of the People, Blood of the Condor, The Traitors, Memories of Underdevelopment,* and *John Reed: Insurgent.* We urge the reader to try to see the many pertinent films made available by the Third World Cinema Group in New York City.

As power seems to become increasingly more concentrated in the hands of a few groups, many of which are multinational or conglomerates, it is imperative that we recognize what we are supporting by our work-a-day commitments to the organizations we serve. *It Is Not Enough Just to Pray* teaches us that the options are indeed narrow but that the work of liberation comes down to personal choices. There are those who are in the precritical state; others are in the critical stage; some are in a highly radicalized postcritical stage of revolutionary commitment, e.g., the directors of *The Hour of the Furnaces* and *The Battle of Chile*, a documentary about the fall of Allende's constitutional regime of democratic socialism. The philosopher Socrates observed long ago: "The unexamined life is not worth living." In a world where institutions more and more impinge on personal life, this axiom has wider implications, for it means we must have knowledge of forces, decisions, and socio-economic dynamics. Latin American films are an excellent complement to what most Americans and Europeans see on the large screen and, indeed, even on the small TV screen.

NOTES

1. This impression is borne out in more scholarly fashion by Professor Charles W. Anderson in his study: "Bankers as Revolutionaries: Politics and Development Banking in Mexico," *The Political Economy of Mexico*, ed. William P. Glade and Charles W. Anderson (Madison: The University of Wisconsin University Press, 1968), pp. 105–85.

2. Horacio Serrano, "Cantinflas," *El Mercurio*, June 24, 1974.

3. James T. Wooten, "Capital Film Festival Opens to 'Dispute,' " *New York Times*, April 4, 1973.

4. George Gent, "Film Critics Score Withdrawal of 'Siege' From Fete," *New York Times*, April 6, 1973.

5. Paulo Freire, *The Pedagogy of the Oppressed* (New York: Herder and Herder, 1971), pp. 45ff.

6. The philosophy of "guerrilla filmmaking" is amply explained by the directors Fernando Solanas and Octavio Getino in their book *Cine, cultura y descolonización* (Buenos Aires: Siglo Veintiuno Argentina Editores S.A., 1973). See Solanas and Getino, "Toward the Third Cinema," *Cineaste*, vol. 4, no. 3 (Winter 1970–71).

7. Latin American films as a contribution to a liberating film humanism are discussed in my book: *Cine: El nuevo humanismo* (Buenos Aires: Búsqueda, 1974).

8.

Liberation and the Future

The ancient Greeks believed that we backed into the future, that it came into view as does the landscape when we ride backwards on a slow-moving train. Persons dedicated to liberation projects prefer to design a future rather than allow it to appear in a random unplanned way. The attitude to the future is very much involved with whether comprehensive anticipatory planning affects our position in the social universe. The periodic meetings of the United Nations Conference on Trade and Development (UNCTAD) and the 1977 North-South Conference in Paris dramatically point up the differences in demands. The industrial democracies generally pledge millions of dollars for annual foreign aid while the developing nations demand better prices for their raw materials and a new international economic order. Even the Soviet Union, concerned about China and militant countries such as India and Algeria, is willing to accommodate the status quo by détente agreements with the U.S.

Liberation theology and a cinema of liberation do not sympathize with the conservative ancient Greek view of the future, which implies that the past is all-determining in our perceptions of reality. Gustavo Gutiérrez has made clear in *A Theology of Liberation*

128

that the utopian dimension cannot ignore the present reality, which is a residual accumulation of historic choices and missed opportunities.[1] Pitirim A. Sorokin, the late Harvard sociologist, forecast a creative future, heralding "the end of a brilliant six hundred-year-long sensate day."[2] For Sorokin, Western culture has been dominated by pragmatic and material considerations to the neglect of supersensory values.

Is Sorokin correct in his optimistic forecast? Does not most science fiction project technologically controlled societies where culture and community are in decided shortfall?

George Orwell, in his uncanny novel *1984*, showed how oppressive the future would be. The British made a very creditable movie of Orwell's book with two stars, the English Michael Redgrave and the American Edmond O'Brien. The latter plays the rebel in a totalitarian state where the government "Big Brother" closely watches every move of its citizens; the former is a police-state official whose duty it is to discourage deviant behavior, such as falling in love, thinking thoughts of dissent, or in any way not showing complete and unquestioning loyalty to "Big Brother." How difficult liberation is in a state where controls extend to electronic means of surveillance, torture, and spy networks is made clear in *1984*. The budding dissenter (played by O'Brien) finally ends by loving "Big Brother" with tears of happiness streaming down his cheeks over the thought of the benevolence of this welfare state. Behavior modification and operant conditioning, as suggested by B. F. Skinner, are growing more popular in urban-technological societies. So too are electronic "bugging," the "newspeak," and stratagems designed to induce forgetting by an historical amnesia through an exaggerated emphasis on today's trends and tomorrows fashions—all

characteristic of Orwell's world of tomorrow. Both the
novel and the film have an awesome reality when we
compare the major traits outlines with our society so
swiftly moving toward 1984 not only in terms of calendar
time but its societal implications.

The challenge of liberation comes from the fact that
technological and scientific power warps our scale of
values. There is something Faustian about the efficiency temptation. If, as Marshall McLuhan has untir-
ingly told us, media technology is an extension of the
human sensorium, then to the extent that satellites, TV,
radio, and film are controlled by a relatively small
number of people, the risk arises that these people will
also have control of public opinion and of the human
mind. Henry Kissinger is reported to have said that
power is an aphrodisiac: It creates moods and states of
mind that the bulk of humanity never experience. The
films of the future give us a sense of this Faustian head-
iness, as if there were some irresistible urge to experiment with every technical possibility that exists. *The
Terminal Man* (1974), starring George Segal, is a dramatic example of this. Segal plays an experimental
guinea pig with cathodes in his brain which permit a
team of technicians and scientists to program him according to whatever emotion or mood or behavior pattern they desire. The most chilling scene in the film is
that in which the "terminal man" is interviewed by a
pretty nurse. In the control room above, hermetically
sealed off from the subject, are the experimenters. They
control the switch connected to the electrodes im-
planted in the experimentee's head. Now he feels depressed; now he feels passionate; now he breaks out into
uncontrollable laughter. His moods are dependent upon
the whim of the control group who observe his actions as
if he were some giant marionette being manipulated
by invisible wires. *The Terminal Man* is a disturbing

film—another in a long list of many that portray negative utopias with little, if any, hope of liberation.

Neither do other futuristic films of the seventies offer much hope: In *Soylent Green*, the teeming masses of New York City are reduced to a synthetic diet in order to survive; in *The Man Who Fell from Earth*, a man from outer space is mistrusted by earth's bureaucratic officialdom and leads a "loveless" existence; in *Logan's Run*, humankind in the twenty-third century is faced with consumer "overchoice"—merely pushing the TV button can introduce into one's living room holographic 3-D personalities; *Brasil 2000* projects the consequences of the present Brazilian form of capitalism—glorious benefits for a military-political-industrial elite and left-overs for the poorer strata of the populace.

As in Hollywood so too in Brazil, Mexico, and India, illusion and distraction serve to veil the more unpleasant social realities that moviegoers see outside the theater. Speaking of Hollywood, film critic Parker Tyler has aptly said: "As a machine, it is wonderfully human; as humanity, it is awesomely mechanical."[3] Science fiction films invariably mechanize existence and present totalitarian scenarios. Let us look at some celluloid projections of "negative utopias."

In John Boorman's *Zardoz* (1974), Sean Connery plays Zed, a fearless "James Bond-type" mortal who visits a nonrepressive society of advanced immortals (called Eternals) and conquers them. The theme is reminiscent of the brutal conquest of the Incas and the Aztecs by Pizarro and Cortes. Conquerors and conquered are mutually transformed. One learns culture and refinement; the subdued are taught violence, sex, and death. The Eternals explore Zed's mind and watch the parade of his memories: images of rape, murder, and intrigue such as we see in popular TV programs. The key image is the crystal that provides order and predictability. As

Marsha Kinder pointed out in an illuminating review in *Film Quarterly:*

Boorman is attacking a utopia like Skinner's *Walden Two,* which, in trying to control behavior and minimize risk and pain, actually eliminates the possibilities for growth and intensity. . . . The Eternals live in a nonsexist, classless, communal society; why should these characteristics necessarily be associated with sterility and a loss of humanity? Only because Boorman imposes the connection. . . . My response to *Zardoz* is paradoxical. I admire the visual artistry but reject the fascist vision.[4]

Zardoz has been compared to Kubrick's *Clockwork Orange* (1972), for both films seem to incline to an authoritarian fascism rather than a grey world of egalitarian socialism. The charming antihero of *Clockwork Orange,* Alex (Roddy MacDowell), and his "droogs" beat and rape at random because their culture is boring. Aggression always culminates in murder. Arrested, Alex is conditioned by methods as violent as his own. Kubrick's film version of Anthony Burgess's story shows that civilization is no longer an operative influence to restrain eroticism or violence. The civil libertarian writer in the film is opposed to the ruling party and so takes up the cudgel against Alex's loss of free will by state conditioning—until he discovers that Alex was his wife's assailant (raping her to the tune of "Singin' in the Rain"). Alex even takes pleasure in the violent and erotic portions of the Bible and he loves Beethoven, whom Kubrick links with Hitler and the Nazis.

No book on liberation and film would be complete without alluding to Jean Luc Godard, who has confined himself to small audiences and low budget films, thus permitting a liberty of expression rarely found in world cinema since the days of Chaplin and Flaherty. Godard has followed the advice of Michelangelo: "He who walks

behind others will never advance." Of him film critic
Pauline Kael has said: No one can follow him because
"he's burned up the ground." The secret of Godard's
prophetic art is that he has opened a window on the
future of western civilization, bringing out the meretri-
cious commercialism, violence, and alienation so we can
see these features of our technocratic societies. Godard
startles us with his sharp dichotomies: Marx or Coca-
Cola. He is a product of the new sensibilities born
after World War II: existentialism, electronic "mind-
expansiveness," and pacifism. In a sense, he is always
making the same film: western people impaled on the
"throw-awayable" comforts of a synthetic civilization
with an escalator standard of living, either socialist or
capitalist. Godard gives us depressing locales: dreary
avenues, uninspiring rivers and canals, empty lots, the
grey Paris banlieu.

In *La Chinoise* (1967) Godard recounts the life of a
small group of Marxist-Leninist militants who pass a
summer in a flat lent by a girl whose parents are away.
We see the cell at work planning violence, discussing
ideological fine points, excluding reformists, critiquing
their own motives, involved in the Vietnam issue. The
girl goes on a terrorist expedition to assassinate an important Soviet figure. By mixing fiction and documentary (the Vietnam war shots are a type of reportage), the
author-director pulls the audience into an alien world.
Other directors break the cinema spell with the appearance of "END" on the screen. For Godard, on the other
hand, lack of continuity and showing the film clapper
boy and the camera crew create the appearance of chaos
but achieve their effects.

In *Alphaville* (1969), Godard takes us to the land of
tomorrow in the shape of another planet. Actually the
entire film was shot in Paris from different angles and

using light and shadow techniques. We see efficiency and rigorous social control. Sexual services in the hotel are standard just as gas, electricity, or water would be. Moreover in *Alphaville* killing for sport is permitted just as in Giermo Petri's *The Tenth Victim*. Godard gives the impression that we are in an Orwellian world where strategy takes the form of language, competition, advertising, and eroticism: where Frenchmen act as if they would be willing "to kill for a Maserati, to go to war for a brassiere Rosy, or to sell female customers a slip Raoul." In short, the energies of members of consumer society are not cooperative but rather antagonistic with contracts, credit, and capital as the tools of motivation for bringing about social harmony.

The most shocking peek at the future was Godard's *Weekend* (1969). A bourgeois couple start on a weekend trip in order to obtain money from the girl's mother. On the way "accordion" smash-ups of cars take place with irate drivers, honking horns, traffic jams, burning cars, and bodies strewn about. Interspersed are sexually stimulating flashbacks of the wife's extramarital affairs, a pianist playing Mozart at a country farm, a garbage truck with a black and Algerian driver each addressing the audience, the throat-cutting of a pig, and the decapitation of a goose. The final scene is the most horrifying: A group of "hippies" are seen eating human flesh in a cannibalistic orgy. The scene is reminiscent of Hieronymus Bosch and has no peer in the history of cinema. It is a preview of hell. Godard has since repudiated his films and has become a revolutionary "purist."

Perhaps the most important technology in shaping the future will be the computer. Today we know that there are advanced computers that can stimulate the decision-making capability of managers of middle-size enterprises. The components are at hand to create thinking machines, either robots that can match human beings in intellectual prowess or hominoids that are simulacra of human beings. The most artistic film ever made about the computerized machine was Stanley Kubrick's *Space Odyssey: 2001*, based on Arthur C. Clarke's screenplay. The film has a stunning beginning, showing the dawn of human life and the ambivalence of tools. When the first higher primate fashions a tool of bone to kill for food and for defense, it throws the instrument in the air. As it descends in slow motion, it turns into a space ship. The tool-making animal is also the space-exploring animal. Not only do human beings voyage into extraterrestrial frontiers out of curiosity but also to stake out claims for their countries as military outposts. Kubrick and Clarke indicate that the American-Soviet rivalry will last into the next century.

The space terminal is studied, with services provided by corporations whose names we recognize: Howard Johnson, Bell Telephone, IBM. If there is any liberation, the multinational corporate structure will not be substantially affected by it. The environment is barren: metallic and stark. The still photo from *2001* bristles with sanitized sterility. The space vessel is manned by two astronauts, played by Gary Lockwood and Keir Dullea. Other astronauts are asleep in "deep freeze." The central figure is HAL, the robot computer who can converse with the crew and even play chess with them. HAL's electronic eye reads the lips of the two astronauts while they are consulting together. HAL is capable of independent judgment, which is why the two crew members are concerned about his loyalty. HAL manages to lock out the two astronauts when they leave the space capsule to repair a faulty part. One drifts out into the boundless reaches of space, while the other

(Keir Dullea) survives, re-enters the vessel, and disrupts the circuits of HAL, who has cut off the life-support system of the frozen crew members. Alone, the sole survivor continues on to Jupiter. The ending of the film is mystical, with the astronaut meeting himself as an aged, dying man. The final cosmic embryo suggests rebirth in consciousness; this is the underlying theme of the movie, as suggested by the floating monolith that mysteriously appears each time there is a quantum leap in human consciousness.

Space Odyssey: 2001 is not as univocally pessimistic as the majority of science fiction movies about the future (e.g., *Metropolis, Modern Times, Fahrenheit 451, The Day the World Caught Fire, On the Beach, Seconds, Sleeper*). There is the suggestion of a "new person," which is the recurring theme in all liberation literature. However the consciousness-raising suggested by Kubrick and Clarke is evolutionary and not revolutionary. The same masters of the world exist and the same private centers of power. The mind-binding assumptions that prevent people from freeing themselves from the shackles of false consciousness are still present.

In Kubrick's other two futuristic films we see the same fatal resignation to human nature as incorrigible, unregenerative. In *Dr. Strangelove, or How I came to Love the Bomb* (1964), Kubrick treats the irrationality in the climate of mutual suspicion between the two major nuclear powers and the basic helplessness of political and military leaders in the face of awesome destructive power. We see Kubrick's pessimism clearly in *Clockwork Orange*. When the rapist gang leader is captured, the state renders him docile by conditioning him to feel intense pain when he hears Beethoven or is exposed to sexual temptation. In showing operant conditioning in its most absurd and inhumane forms, the film ends, as

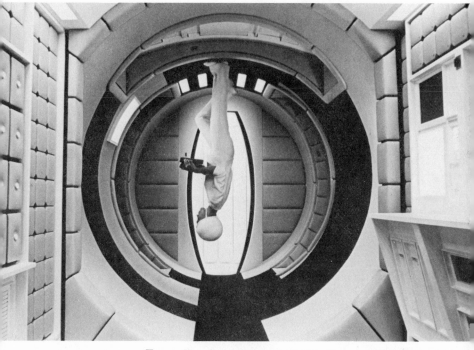

From Stanley Kubrick's 2001: Space Odyssey

From the MGM release 2001: A SPACE ODYSSEY
© 1968 Metro-Goldwyn-Mayer Inc.

does Costa Gavras's *State of Siege*, with grave doubts about the betterment of the human species. Kubrick is a liberal and basically takes his clues from the past. He as yet has not shown himself capable of utopian thinking. The doubts raised by the science fiction future-oriented films treated in this chapter do not add up to a liberation model. But they are the first steps toward conscientization and, from there, to an "anti-project."

In Francois Truffaut's screen version of Bradbury's *Fahrenheit 451* (1966) we have an "anti-project." When the fireman (Oskar Werner) discovers that the books he and his colleagues burn contain dissenting—and therefore liberating—thoughts, he escapes the electronic totalitarian regime he has so uncritically been serving to join other refugees in a camp where each is assigned to memorize some great work of literature. Liberation is a matter of alternatives, not merely—as in the works of Stanley Kubrick—an unmasking of the pretensions of society and its citizens.

In *Toward a Film Humanism* (New York: Delta pbk., 1975), I proposed some insights with regard to the future. Human beings and technology, it seems, are indissolubly wedded, so that large-scale organizations, the precondition for any scientific advance, will be part of future scenarios, with bureaucratic specialization as a basic way of life for twenty-first-century humankind. Furthermore there is the danger of reductionism, that is to say, the predominance of measurable goals of a quantitative nature rather than a consideration of spiritual factors that escape empirical criteria. The human-machine interface will remain with us if motion pictures and the imagination of our best science fiction writers are any test of reliability. Computers, television, satellites, and lasers will constitute a new technological nervous system for the human race. As Pierre Teilhard de Chardin said in *The Phenomenon of Man*, the discovery of the electromagnetic spectrum was a biological event.

Kenneth Boulding has perceptively pointed out that the fundamental dynamic in social systems is the human learning process. In this not only is information important, but also value-orientation—what we call "conscientization," the ordered knowledge of how social structures work and how the lines of force benefit some and disadvantage others. We must guard against a future that is illusory—merely an imaginary escape into a rosy world we think will get better. The process of liberation must have "fail-safe" mechanisms to protect against such false conceptions of utopian thought. A study of futuristic films is a valuable source of insight into the high probability that tomorrow's world will not be any different—perhaps it will be even more oppressive—than today's society unless there are effective strategies of change and tactics of liberation. We do not need more confirmation of how weak people are. What is needed are examples of courageous liberation efforts that do not seek power in order to oppress in a different manner but rather to redistribute power and opportunity for the purpose of a fuller humanization of the planet. Otherwise, to quote Godard, the planet will be divided into equally alienating systems governed by totalitarian Marxism or the Coca-colonization process of the market system.

The movies examined are signposts to the perils of imagining that any appreciable change in the major directions of contemporary world society is imminent. This should not lead to discouragement, however; personal liberation is always possible, as Robert Bresson and Carl Dreyer, the screen's most spiritual directors, have shown in their films. There are some excellent movies regarding such personal liberation and conversion: *The Birdman of Alcatraz, Lonely Are the Brave, The Pawnbroker, On the Waterfront, Patterns, Man in the Gray Flannel Suit*, and the Japanese *High and Low* by Akira Kurosawa. But what is needed is for like-minded persons to band together in some "anti-project" that assures an alternate lifestyle characterized by choices not feasible in the dominant culture. Of the films considered in this chapter, only *Fahrenheit 451* portrayed such a group effort at liberation from "Big Brother." As a giant Rorschach test to see whether the future will be humanizing or not, science-fiction motion pictures are largely discouraging.[5] However this should only increase the degree of realism in our thinking. Utopian thinking, to be truly liberating, must not overlook the high probability scenarios.

Daniel Berrigan has aptly said that the costs of being a human being are going up with each passing year. *Star Wars* apart, sci-fi movies prove this: *Alphaville, 1984, Space Odyssey: 2001, Metropolis, Seconds, The Terminal Man, The Tenth Victim, Weekend*, and *Rollerball*. The Apocalypse for Christians is a book of divine revelation; nonetheless, not a few Christians shy away from the flaming finale portrayed there. Liberation is too serious for thinking thoughts only of positive utopia; to be genuine, it must also come to grips with the less reassuring thoughts of "negative utopias." Aldous Huxley so well said about his last years in California: "I have seen the future and it doesn't work! " The challenge of liberation is never over, whether at the personal or social level. All alternatives must be considered: the least probable and the most probable, the least consoling and the most promising.

NOTES

1. Gustavo Gutiérrez, *A Theology of Liberation*, trans. Sister Caridad Inda and John Eagleson (Maryknoll, N.Y.: Orbis Books, 1971), p. 233.

2. P. Sorokin, *The Crisis of Our Age* (New York: E.P. Dutton & Co., 1941), p. 13.

3. Parker Tyler, *The Hollywood Hallucination* (New York: Simon and Schuster, 1944), p. 11.

4. Marsha Kinder, "Zardoz," *Film Quarterly*, Summer 1974, pp. 56–57.

5. David Amman, *Catastrophe: The End of the Cinema?* (New York: Bounty Books, 1975).

9.

Suggestions for Film Studies on Human Liberation Themes

Motion pictures, as commercial enterprises, are geared to pleasing mass audiences. There is a sense in which they tend to mute social criticism and to reinforce the status quo, as the well-known sociologists Robert Merton and Paul Lazarsfeld indicated many years ago.[1] Nevertheless, there is an irrepressible urge among artists to treat bold themes, even at the risk of box-office failure. Chaplin, as we saw, succeeded in gaining a global following, particularly among the underprivileged, by means of his "little tramp" persona. In the silent era, D. W. Griffith, Erich von Stroheim, Josef von Sternberg, Robert Flaherty, and King Vidor raised consciousness in such films as *Birth of a Nation, Intolerance, Broken Blossoms* (Griffith), *Blind Husbands, Foolish Wives, The Wedding March, Greed* (von Stroheim), *The Docks of New York, Underworld* (von Sternberg), *Nanook of the North, Moana, Tabu* (Flaherty), and *The Big Parade, The Crowd, Hallelujah!* (Vidor).

The sound era was ushered in by Warner Brothers' use of the Vitaphone technique in *The Jazz Singer* (1927), starring Al Jolson. Sound films whet the appetite of

142

Americans for movies (100 million went each week in 1930; the United States had a population of only 120 million at that time). Josef von Sternberg filmed Theodore Dreiser's fictional analysis of social stratification, *An American Tragedy* (1931), a story of a working-class boy who gets a factory girl pregnant and then tries to kill her after he falls in love with the daughter of the factory owner. Sound made the tragedy more eloquent since the dialogue was full of promises, contradictions, and ironies. One film writer described the film as "a steady and derisive gaze at the U.S.A.'s departure from the Lincoln principle that 'all men are created equal.' " Furthermore, new film genres appeared due to sound: the gangster film (the staccato effect of machine guns and the clipped speech of the urban hoodlums); the "dance film" (with Busby Berkeley's lavishly choreographed musicals and the dancing feet of Fred Astaire and Ginger Rogers); the zany comedies seasoned with the fast repartee of Clark Gable, Cary Grant, Groucho Marx, W. C. Fields, Carole Lombard, Rosalind Russell, Mae West.

Mention should be made of one studio that took social themes more seriously than its rivals: Warner Brothers, which had launched the "talkie." It began to mix entertainment with liberation themes in a very subtle but highly effective way. Such an assertion may surprise many film critics and buffs, but there is a reason for it. In his *Essay on Liberation*, Herbert Marcuse has perceptively observed that a change in sensibility is a political factor, that the senses must be enlisted to help the imagination to produce "the images of freedom."[2] Whereas Metro-Goldwyn-Mayer, Radio Keith-Orpheum (R.K.O.), Paramount, and Twentieth Century-Fox went in for fantasy, escapism, and "pure entertainment," Warner Brothers pursued realism as a production policy. Jack Warner, the most important of the four Warner Brothers, ran the studio as a newspaper editor, demanding from his writers that they deliver stories with a "news peg": fast-paced dramas that reflected the headlines of the thirties, streaked with violence, conflict, injustice, love, and human interest. The Warner Brothers produced highly atmospheric films in which deviants and socially marginal people were portrayed in an unprecedentedly sympathetic light. James Cagney, Edward G. Robinson, Humphrey Bogart, and Paul Muni might be jailed, hunted, or even killed, but the audience felt that they were victims of circumstances beyond their control, that if the historical cards were different, they might have been upstanding, even outstanding, citizens.

The most obvious film in the series of "social crime-theory" motion pictures produced by Warners was *Angels with Dirty Faces*. The movie opens with two boys running away from the police: One trips and is apprehended and the other escapes. The latter grows up to become a Catholic priest (Pat O'Brien); the former goes to reform school and becomes a criminal (James Cagney). The film ends with the priest explaining to some worshipful youngsters in his parish (played by the Dead End Kids) that he could have become like his childhood friend, who had just been executed in the electric chair for a murder he committed to protect the priest. The mitigating tribute he pays goes like this: "Here's to a boy that couldn't run as fast as I could!"

Any viewing of Warner Brothers' movies made in the Depression Era will reveal the unusual approach of that studio in trying to offset the long-standing Calvinist tradition in America that the poor, the unemployed, and the deviant—not society—were responsible for their situation. The underlying assumptions of films from

Warner Brothers were those derived from the Chicago school of sociology (Parks, Sutherland, etc.) and can be seen to best advantage in several films frequently shown on TV reruns: *I Was a Fugitive from a Chain Gang, Little Caesar, Public Enemy, Marked Woman, San Quentin, Knock on any Door, Bullets or Ballots, The Amazing Dr. Clitterhouse, They Won't Forget, Black Fury,* and *Brother Orchid.* Warners also treated the theme of deviant intellectuals and national leaders: *Juarez, The Story of Louis Pasteur, The Life of Emile Zola, Dr. Ehrlich's Magic Bullet, Dispatch from Reuters.* All these films treated social change and risk-taking to better social and economic conditions.

Although Warner Brothers specialized in films that focused on society as the villain rather than on the deviant person, the rival studios did not completely neglect social themes, as in *Manhattan Melodrama, Scarface, Our Daily Bread, The Prisoner of Shark Island, Make Way for Tomorrow, The Grapes of Wrath, Dead End, Street Scene, Fury,* and *You Only Live Once.*

The daring themes of the social-consciousness films, pioneered mainly by Warner Brothers, decreased as the New Deal period matured and the shadows of World War II lengthened over America. Frank Capra deserves a special niche in this chapter on liberation films. No single director so epitomizes the Hollywood era of the thirties as does Capra, and no one so portrayed the American dream and devotion to the "common man" more unswervingly or more artistically than he. His philosophy has been called a "fantasy of goodwill," but this is to overlook his profound grasp of the uniqueness of the American way or life. (He was born in Sicily and chanced into the movie industry in a manner worthy of a Horatio Alger story.) True, Capra's best social crusading movies are dated, as are the films of other nativist

directors who were dedicated to themes of Americana:
D. W. Griffith, Henry King, King Vidor, John Ford,
Frank Borzage, and "Woody" Van Dyke. Nevertheless,
he put his finger on the soft spot of corruptibility in
America with films such as *Mr. Smith Goes to Washington, Meet John Doe, Mr. Deeds Goes to Town*, and *It's a
Wonderful Life*. Ralph Nader is straight out of a Capra
movie; so too are Jimmy Carter and Jerry Brown. All
resemble those archetypal Capra heroes, protrayed by
James Stewart and Gary Cooper, who pursued lofty civic
ideals in the face of great odds—veritable Davids fighting the political and corporate Goliaths. Capra appreciated, as no American director since his time, how
the acids of acquisitiveness could corrode the structures
of the nation's political freedoms.

The Roosevelt era of U.S. cinema ended with the appearance of the first Hollywood screen rebel—John Garfield, who played a remarkable role as the "born loser"
in a movie about a small town family (*Four Daughters*).
In Garfield's persona, the protest was not directed out-
wardly. In this Garfield differed from earlier rebel
types. James Cagney, Edward G. Robinson, Paul Muni,
and Spencer Tracy (in his early roles) showed aggressive
hostility by saying "No" to the traditional Ameri-
canism. Instead, Garfield struck a strange psychological
pose in which protest was muted into a style of one who
knew all, who saw through society but who was going to
live his life despite the tilts and biases in society. The
rebel pose would become especially popular in the forties as World War II changed American sensibilities.[3]

Humphrey Bogart is the classic exponent of the exis-
tentialist "loner" in whom the French saw incarnated
the writings of Jean Paul Sartre and Albert Camus.
Alan Ladd was another rebel whose strength lay in his
inwardness and reticence. Bogart can be seen at his best
in *Casablanca, The Maltese Falcon, The Big Sleep*, and

To Have and to Hold. In the last two films, Lauren Bacall is co-featured, presenting a new type of liberated, self-resourceful woman. Veronica Lake was another such type and often played opposite Alan Ladd (e.g., *This Gun for Hire*). Liberation was suggested to be more psychological than political, more a matter of personal insight than mass movements.

Some remarkable films were made in the forties. In addition to its path-breaking cinematic techniques, Orson Welles's *Citizen Kane* demonstrates a profound understanding of social ascent and influence-peddling in American society. It is well-known that the film was inspired by the career of William Randolph Hearst, who used his mining fortune to affect public opinion and national issues in journalism, electoral politics, and even moviemaking.[4] Darryl Zanuck, a movie mogul who served his apprenticeship at Warner Brothers, produced *Gentleman's Agreement* and *Pinky*, both significant message movies on racism. The latter treated the black issue, while the former confronted anti-Semitism in America. Elia Kazan directed *Pinky* and brought an instinct for social realism to Hollywood with films such as *A Tree Grows in Brooklyn*, *Boomerang*, and *Panic in the Streets*.

Another frank look at American bigotry (i.e., anti-Semitism) was *Crossfire*, directed by Edward Dymtryk. Dymtryk was one of the Hollywood ten, that blacklisted group of directors, producers, scenarists, and attorneys who refused to "name names" or cooperate in any way with the House Committee on Un-American Activities (HUAC) in its dogged pursuit of Communist infiltration of the U.S. motion picture industry.[5] The background of this period, with its obsessive anti-Communist witch-hunt, can be seen in *The Way We Were*, starring Barbra Streisand and Robert Redford, and in *The Front*, starring Zero Mostel and Woody Allen. It is interesting how throughout U.S. history the fear of new ideas reasserts itself.[6]

It is hard to inventory the suffering and injustice brought about by the HUAC investigation. The cold wind of suspicion blew across Hollywood, estranging friends and sowing mistrust. Myrna Loy was held suspect because of her friendship with Mrs. Eleanor Roosevelt. John Garfield's premature death by heart attack cannot be completely divorced from his deep involvement in the HUAC investigations. Elia Kazan cooperated with the committee and was criticized by those who did not. Kazan went on to distinguish himself in the fifties with a number of remarkable films with social themes, such as *A Streetcar Named Desire, On the Waterfront*, and *Viva Zapata!* However, Kazan's critics feel that he portrays betrayers as heroes (e.g., Marlon Brando's role in *On the Waterfront*) and the people as basically incapable of staging a successful revolt (e.g., Marlon Brando's role as the tragic rebel leader in *Viva Zapata!*). Kazan fluctuated between psychological analyses (*East of Eden, Baby Doll*) and social critiques, (*Wild River, Face in the Crowd*). His social signature wavered—understandably.

Movies in the fifties began to probe into American history and institutions. Director William Wyler did justice to Theodore Dreiser's *Carrie* (1951), but the film failed at the box-office. *All the King's Men* looked at political demagoguery à la Huey Long. *The Big Carnival, The Great Man*, and *Sweet Smell of Success* criticized the mass media. *Death of a Salesman* was a more searing indictment of the hidden personal costs of our merchandising mores than *The Hucksters* (1947), which starred Clark Gable. Military life was closely examined in *Paths of Glory, From Here to Eternity*, and *Stalag 17. Broken Arrow* was Hollywood's first pro-Indian movie.[7] *The Man with a Golden Arm*, starring Frank Sinatra as a "junkie" gambler, was the first film to look at drug addiction. Corporations came in for searching cinematic examination in *Executive Suite, The Man in the Grey Flannel Suit, A Woman's World, Patterns*, and *Cash McCall*. Working conditions were elemental in the plots of *The Whistle at Eaton Falls, Salt of the Earth* (by Herbert Biberman, one of the blacklisted "Hollywood Ten"), *On the Waterfront, I Can Get It for You Wholesale*, and *The Garment Jungle*. Hollywood looked at itself in *The Big Knife, Sunset Boulevard, The Bad and the Beautiful, The Goddess*, and *A Star is Born*.

New stars such as Marilyn Monroe, Judy Holiday, Jack Lemmon, Doris Day, Rock Hudson, and Jerry Lewis were different than the stars of the thirties: They were "trendy," at times neurotic, typical of the "other-directed" character described in David Riesman's *The Lonely Crowd*. These stars can be studied in films which show the new consumeristic mood of the U.S. in the fifties: *The Marrying Kind, It Should Happen to You, Artist and Models, Cinderfella, The Bellboy, The Solid Gold Cadillac, Divorce American Style, Pillow Talk*, and *Days of Wine and Roses*. Paddy Chayefsky brought his television scripting skills to Hollywood and studied the plight of the small man caught in the toils of a complex urban-technological society in *Marty, Bachelor Party, The Catered Affair*, and *Middle of the Night*. Although the principal focus of many of these films is personal and psychological, the reader who is attentive to our model of human liberation can deduce social lessons from the plots of these movies. A new "consumer-oriented" America emerges from the images of *The Seven Year Itch, Boy's Night Out, Breakfast at Tiffany's, Madison Avenue, Man from the Diner's Club, The Apartment*, and *The Carpetbaggers*.

Special mention should be made of James Dean and his role in *Rebel Without a Cause*. In his persona, the electrifying young actor—who later died racing his Porsche Snyder on the road between Monterey and Salinas, California—combined traits of Cagney, Bogart, Garfield, and Brando. In *Rebel Without a Cause*, he crystallized the smouldering discontent of U.S. youth in the Age of Anxiety, the age of the "organization man," of sexual awakening (the Kinsey reports), and of Riesman's "other-directedness." The U.S. family and U.S. youth have never been the same since the Eisenhower period. The counterculture of the sixties, the passage of the nuclear family to the atomistic family with members seeking greater fulfillment outside the home, the bondage of women to the suburban family —all these phenomena are foreshadowed in Nicholas Ray's powerful film, *Rebel Without a Cause*, as well as in *The Wild One*, *Blackboard Jungle*, and *The Young Strangers*. The shift in perception, which Marshall McLuhan attributes to movies, TV, and pictorial journalism, was dramatized in these films of the fifties. Perhaps the deepest revolution is that of perception. This is the "revolutionary revolution"; all others are secondary, though important.

The sweeping tide of youthful protest, triggered by *Rebel Without a Cause*, reached England (the "teddy boys"), France ("les blousons noirs"), Italy ("gioventù bruciata"), and even Russia ("stalyagi"). James Dean's style, also seen in *East of Eden* and *Giant*, was an example of charisma. Writing of James Dean in his book *Mid-Century*, the late John Dos Passos said of him: "The teenagers approved: 'Everything he said was cool.' "[8] Later, in France, Jean Luc Godard would put up the theme of youthful discontent, presenting the dilemma of youth as poised between consumer capitalism and communist "totalism" in *Masculine-Feminine*. Godard's subtitle for this film was very expressive: "The Children of Marx and Coca-Cola."

The revolution that Dean initiated in the tradition of Cagney, Bogart, Garfield, and Brando was continued by the Beatles, whose magnetic hold over teenage audiences can be seen in *A Hard Day's Night* and *Help!* Some have held that the crowd euphoria of the young in the age of "rock 'n' roll" masks fascist tendencies. What promises liberation may often bring another, perhaps more complete, form of authoritarian control. Some excellent films were made in the sixties about this totalitarian potential in youthful ecstasy: *Wild in the Streets, Privilege, Expresso Bongo*, documentaries such as *Monterey Pop, Gimme Shelter, Woodstock, The Groupies*, and cinéma-vérité features of Bob Dylan (*Don't Look Back!*), the Rolling Stones, and Janis Joplin. We should mention films that dealt with campus protest (*Getting Straight, The Strawberry Statement, The Activist*, and *RPM*) and the "now movies," which heralded the arrival of a new consciousness in the mid- and late sixties, when filmmakers realized that those under twenty-five years of age made up the bulk of the movie audience. To understand the liberation process that has gone on since *Rebel Without a Cause*, attention should be paid to films such as *Bonnie and Clyde, The Graduate, Easy Rider, Hi! Mom, Greetings, Five Easy Pieces, Drive, He Said, Two-Lane Blacktop, Midnight Cowboy, M.A.S.H.*, and *Zabriskie Point*.

Movies have especially reflected and helped to produce notable changes in the position of women in society: Cher in *Chastity*, Dyan Cannon in *Bob and Carol and Ted and Alice*, Liza Minnelli in *The Sterile Cuckoo*, Candice Bergen in *Carnal Knowledge*, Jane Fonda in *Barefoot in the Park, Any Wednesday, Sunday in New*

York, *Klute*, Cicely Tyson in *Sounder*, Carrie Snodgrass in *Diary of a Mad Housewife*, Diane Keaton in *The Godfather*, Mia Farrow in *John and Mary*, Goldie Hawn in *Cactus Flower*, Shirley MacLaine in *Two for the Seesaw*, Raquel Welch in *Myra Breckinridge*, Diahann Carroll in *Claudine*, Ellen Burstyn in *Alice Doesn't Live Here Anymore*, Gena Rowlands in *Woman Under the Influence*, and Katherine Ross in *The Stepford Wives*. People who wish to understand better the feminist movement should take movies seriously.[9] The same can be said for understanding the position of homosexuals: *The Killing of Sister George*, *Secret Ceremony*, *Theresa and Isabel*, *The Odd Couple*, *The Staircase*, *Reflections in a Golden Eye*, *The Servant*, and *Boys in the Band*. As for race, Sidney Poitier has helped to raise consciousness with such films as *Pressure Point*, *Lilies of the Field*, *A Patch of Blue*, *Guess Who's Coming to Dinner?*

There is no doubt that the movies of the late sixties and the seventies have widened the perimeters of the "limit-situations" of the tolerance, even the acceptance, of attitudes and behavior patterns regarding sex, race, social class, age, and religion. Even ethnic origins have been treated, especially in presenting the viewpoint of Puerto Ricans as in *West Side Story*, *Popi!* and *The Pawnbroker*. However, there is a dark side to the movies made in America in this period: the increase of violence, of cynicism, and of a vigilante attitude whereby "law-and-order" officials, despairing of justice in the courts, take matters into their own hands. These symptoms point to a fascist tendency, a totalitarian syndrome. Even John Ford abandoned his earlier nostalgic treatment of the West (e.g., *Stagecoach*, *My Darling Clementine*, and *Wagonmaster*) to indulge in a harsher, less mythologized, interpretation of frontier life in *The Searchers*, *The Man Who Shot Liberty Valance*, and *Cheyenne Autumn*.

The character of John Wayne changes notably. As Rooster Cogburn in *True Grit*, he disregards the law, triggers his gun, and says, in true vigilante style: "You don't hand a summons to a low-down rat." In *The Cowboys* (1972), John Wayne plays Will Andersen, a rugged trail boss who is deceived by his hired hands when they learn about the gold strike in California. In desperation, Andersen signs on eleven adolescents and teaches them how to rope, ride, and shoot. They learn quickly. When attacked by a gang of desperadoes who kill Andersen, the eleven novice cowpunchers (note the mystical number of the faithful apostles in the Bible) seek revenge. In some of the most chilling scenes ever filmed, savagery by these youths seeking their manhood is passed off as heroic retribution.[10]

Among the films noted for endorsing violence as a solution to problems are *Little Murders*, *The Long Goodbye*, *The Detective* (with Frank Sinatra), the Clint Eastwood "police films" (*Coogan's Bluff*, *Dirty Harry*, *Magnum Force*), *Bullitt*, *The New Centurions*, *Across 110th Street*, and *The French Connection*. Frightening defenses of violence were seen in *Death Wish*, *Taxi Driver*, and *Lipstick*. Sam Peckinpah has been called the lyricist of violence with films such as *The Wild Bunch*, *Straw Dogs*, *The Getaway*, *Pat Garrett and Billy the Kid*, and *Bring Me the Head of Alfredo Garcia*. Filmmakers in America have been intensifying the theme of violence in all the traditional screen genres: thrillers, westerns, science fiction, war films, and disaster movies. A favorite film of mine which reveals widespread social imbalances in America is Sidney Lumet's *Dog Day Afternoon*.

Before we close this chapter, I wish to draw the reader's attention to some films that deserve special consideration in any course on liberation. Let us begin with the unusual cinéma-vérité documentaries of Frederick Wiseman. Wiseman is a lawyer turned filmmaker. Instead of studying personalities, Wiseman studies institutions. His first film, *Law and Order*, focused on police activities in a black ghetto. His *Titicut Follies* took as its theme human degradation in an institution for the criminally insane. Wiseman does not use stereotypes (e.g., sadistic guards), but rather lets the camera speak for itself, thus challenging the spectator to judge in a responsible, generally complex, way. In *High School* viewers are made aware of how seldom they hear the school children talking. The film is funny through its absurdity as boys are taught cooking and girls hang from rings in gym class as instructors shout "Tarzan" and "Super-Tarzan" when they attain appropriate levels of endurance.

In *Hospital*, Wiseman typically places the institution in a setting where larger problems from outside the hospital surface. Doctors make urgent telephone calls to other agencies that neglect their responsibility. The patients are not seldom afflicted by poverty and family neglect. The staff does its best to cope but finds itself in a social morass. Wiseman is a major contributor to a cinematic science of human liberation. In the last scene of *Hospital* patients at a church service put money in a collection plate and sing "Ave Maria." The singing ebbs as the camera lens zooms out and leaves the hospital in the background till we see the high-powered passenger cars speeding on the freeways. Thus Wiseman symbolizes public indifference and makes us see that we are accomplices in the institutional oppression so widespread in our affluent society. As John Kenneth Galbraith pointed out in *The Affluent Society*, ours is a society in which public deprivation exists alongside great private manifestations of wealth.

Another kind of liberation film is that produced by

socialist directors outside the U.S.S.R. The Italian director Luchino Visconti, a Marxist sympathizer, worked in 1936 with Jean Renoir, then the foremost realist of fictional cinema. Visconti went on to direct such powerful films as *Ossessione, Senso, Rocco and His Brothers, The Leopard,* and *The Damned.* Like Renoir (*The Grand Illusion* and *Rules of the Game*), so too Visconti has been concerned with class identity and the differences among humans due to their position in the social universe.

In addition to Visconti, there is the late Italian Marxist director Pier Paolo Pasolini, whose social realism is evident in his earlier work (before *Oedipus Rex* and *120 Days of Sodom*). In *Accatone,* Pasolini showed the squalor of the slums—an unrelenting portrayal of ghetto waste reminiscent of Luis Buñuel's *Los Olvidados.* In *The Gospel According to St. Matthew,* he showed a Christ who was a revolutionary and a defender of the poor against the priestly aristocracy. In *Teorema,* Pasolini showed a mysterious stranger who met the sexual needs of members of a Christian family with decidedly bourgeois yearnings.

Undoubtedly the most exciting socialist director in the West is Lina Wertmuller, whose films treat sex, politics, and cultural patterns with brilliant irony and incisive humor. Her constant theme seems to be that in. the West (specifically Italy) everything is in place but nothing really is in order. This motif that ran through *All Screwed Up* can be discerned in more disciplined form in *The Seduction of Mimi, Love and Anarchy, Swept Away,* and *Seven Beauties.* The still photo from *All Screwed Up* shows a strike of slaughterhouse workers—from which nothing lasting ensues. As communism bids fair to grow electorally in Italy, Wertmuller's films capture the breakdown of feudal religions, family and social (read Mafia) traditions, and the rise of a new criti-

Striking slaughterhouse workers in Lina Wertmuller's All Screwed Up

cal attitude by workers, intellectuals and youth. *1900* by Bernardo Bertolucci analyzes Italian fascism in dramatic epic style.

Cuban cinema has been distinguished by the work of Tomás Gutiérrez Alea, who directed *Memories of Underdevelopment*. He has also directed a film about Cuban revolution, *Historias de la Revolución* (never released in the U.S.), *Death of a Bureaucrat*, and *A Cuban Fight Against the Demons*. Sponsored by the state, Gutiérrez Alea has maintained a remarkable integrity in revealing "the influence of socio-historic forces on human feelings."[11] Americans interested in liberation should make an effort to see representative works of Cuban motion picture directors.

In the mid-seventies the United States has been experiencing a rash of devour-and-disaster films such as *The Poseidon Adventure, Airport 75, The Towering Inferno, Earthquake, The Hindenburg, Willard, Jaws, Grizzly,* and *Squirm*. Surprisingly, these movies are quite revealing. One psychiatrist in California commented in 1975 that they serve as a release for people plagued by the bad news of Watergate, rising prices, taxes, unemployment, and the possibility of Eurocommunism in Spain, Italy, and Portugal. Liberation must not only stay at the political, economic, and social surfaces; it must reach psychic depths. The disaster films, the supernatural films, the horror films that feature family invaders (e.g., *The Omen, Carrie, Burnt Offerings*) reveal a deep psychological malaise in the U.S. people—fear, paranoia, and distrust. Gerald Sykes, a well-known psychologist, has said that the challenge facing the United States is to complete the first revolution in the sphere of political and civil liberties with a psychological revolution whereby we learn to face reality and not live in a state of wishful thinking, whether positive (U.S. advertising) or negative (anti-Communist propaganda). The films about catastrophe, science fiction, and vigilantes are a "pseudo-liberation," giving us a false sense of security in the feeling that things could be worse.[12] The vast popularity of *The Exorcist* suggests that perhaps the U.S. psyche is not capable of facing its inner dreads, its subconscious anxieties.

What will the future bring? Possible destruction through atomic holocaust, or environmental "backlash" through scarce resources, pollution, and overcrowding? These themes run through *Dr. Strangelove, Fail-Safe, The Forbin Project, Planet of the Apes, Solyent Green, Logan's Run,* and *Zardoz.* Other typical plots feature people with a plastic, empty look (e.g., *Alphaville, Sleeper, The Stepford Wives, The Tenth Victim*) or where computers of "robotized" humans abound (e.g., *Clockwork Orange, Space Odyssey: 2001, Seconds, The Terminal Man*). Most futuristic films suggest a dark destiny. George Lucas's *Star Wars* breeds optimism, but the righteousness of such Nordic heroes as Luke Starwalker is troubling. Should the force be with him? Or rather should he be with the force? Some see *Star Wars* as a fascist fable.

I personally find more consolation in Federico Fellini's *La Dolce Vita,* which opens and closes with two symbols of judgment: the statue of Christ with his arms open as it casts shadows on Rome while being borne aloft by a helicopter and, finally, the eye of the giant ray on the beach staring at the revelers at an all-night orgy. The film closes with a shot of Marcello, the weak journalist who cannot resist the lure of his occupation and the "sweet life" with the international jet set. He sees the simple country girl from Umbria; she tries to communicate with him. The roar of the ocean billows prevents him from hearing her. Instead of going toward her he allows himself to be pulled aside by a party girl. The scene leaves us with a strange feeling of hope—that Marcello can find his liberation tomorrow and that grace is always present, beckoning quietly and inviting a free response. There are no facile "happy-endings" in the best liberation movies (e.g., *Open City, Burn!, The Seduction of Mimi, State of Siege*). The struggle in itself attests to hope in utopian alternatives, to the abiding truth that we are here to become, not merely to be.

NOTES

1. Paul F. Lazarsfeld and Robert K. Merton, "Mass Communication, Popular Taste and Organized Social Action," *Mass Communications*, ed. Wilbur Schramm (Urbana, Illinois: University of Illinois Press, 1949), pp. 459–80.

2. Herbert Marcuse, *An Essay on Liberation* (Boston: Beacon Press, 1969), Chap. 2, "The New Sensibility," pp. 23ff.

3. See Joe Morella and Edward Z. Epstein (Introduction by Judith Crist) *Rebels: The Rebel Hero in Films* (New York: Citadel Press, 1971).

4. See the biographical sketch of William Randolph Hearst in Philip French's *The Movie Moguls* (Chicago: Henry Regnery Co., 1969).

5. See Victor S. Navasky, "The Hollywood Ten Recalled: To Name or Not to Name," *The New York Times Magazine*, March 10, 1973, pp. 34ff.

6. "In the decade after the Revolution we passed the Alien and Sedition laws; after the Civil War we abolished eleven states and converted them into military districts; after World War I we staged the Mitchell-Palmer witchhunt; after World War II we set up the Attorney General's subversive list and the theory of guilt by association. In each case the armed enemy had been defeated and the imminent physical danger averted—but then terror possessed us—the psychological fear of conversion—operationally a profound revolt against one of the basic theories of the republic, namely, the safety with which error of opinion may be tolerated where reason is left free to combat it" (Gerald W. Johnson, *The Lunatic Fringe* [Philadelphia: J.B. Lippincott Co., 1957], p. 26).

7. For a thorough study of the unconscious but consistent portrayal of Indians as the enemy, see Ralph and Natasha Friar, *The Only Good Indian: The Hollywood Gospel* (New York: Drama Book Specialists, 1972).

8. John Dos Passos, "The Sinister Adolescents," *Mid-Century* (Boston: Houghton Mifflin Co., 1961), p. 480.

9. An interesting study of the evolution of women's image in

American movies is Jacques Siclier, *Le mythe de la femme dans le cinéma américain* (Paris: Du Cerf, 1956).

10. John Wayne described the character he plays in his one hundred and sixty-second film, *The War Wagon*, as "the big tough boy on the side of right—that's me" (cited by Jerzy Toeplitz in *Hollywood and After: The Changing Face of American Cinema* [London: George Allen and Unwin Ltd., 1974], p. 138).

11. See Margot Kernan, "Cuban Cinema: Tomás Gutiérrez Alea," *Film Quarterly*, Winter 1975–76, pp. 45–52.

12. Vincent Canby, "Cynical Cinema Is Chic," *New York Times*, Arts & Leisure, November 21, 1976.

Epilogue

Movies represent the new humanism, as I argued in *Toward a Film Humanism.* Whether on the small screen of TV or on the large theatre screen equipped with stereophonic sound and technicolor, movies make available to the masses what once was within the reach only of royalty, the aristocracy, and a privileged elite. Not all mass entertainment qualifies as art, to be sure, but within the stream of "sight-sound" images are many currents of tasteful, even inspiring, experiences. Classical scholars tell us that "catharsis," as explained by Aristotle and other commentators on ancient drama, meant not only emotional release but also the pleasure derived from understanding. This recalls Joseph Conrad's boast, later repeated by D. W. Griffith: "My aim is, above all, to make you see." The humanities were always considered "liberating." The thought is almost explicit in the phrase "the liberal arts." Today the film art has brought countless millions, including illiterates, within reach of this type of liberating humanism. For the price of an admission ticket or the twist of the dial of a television receiver, humankind has access to the boundless universe of vicarious experience.

The instant access to movies is a contributing factor toward a global wave of consciousness regarding certain constants of the species—our sense of solidarity, the realization that in our common clay is a spark that unites us at the nonmaterial level of understanding and love. No one proves this more dramatically than Charles Chaplin, who communicated not only joy but also hope to world audiences in this century. Liberation is not exclusively the work of revolutionaries, political activists, and social agitators, though their roles can never be absent. It must be the work of parents, educators, the clergy, the foundations, the artists—and our mass entertainers, who have the gifts and skills to touch the universal chord of empathy in all of us.

And let us make no mistake: Liberation is very much a matter of feeling as well as understanding. I personally confess that my emotional patterns were shaped as a teenager by seeing the Warner Brothers' films that portrayed crusaders like Louis Pasteur, Dr. Ehrlich, Emile Zola, and Benito Juárez, as well as the social conditions that bred crime, social revolt, and ideological deviance from the cherished, often unexamined, belief system of the conforming majority.

We have pointed out numerous examples of entertainment films that can raise consciousness and promote human liberation. The audience feels oppressed and outraged upon seeing *Potemkin, Los Olvidados, The Grapes of Wrath, Phantom India,* and *The Sorrow and the Pity.* The need for human liberation is felt. So too we moviegoers identify with the goals and person of a Gandhi *(Nine Hours to Rama),* a T. E. Lawrence *(Lawrence of Arabia),* a Zapata *(Viva Zapata!),* a Villa *(John Reed: Insurgent),* a Joan of Arc *(The Passion of Joan of Arc),* a José Dolores *(Burn!),* and union reformers portrayed in *The Organizer, Salt of the Earth, On the Waterfront,* and *The Molly Maguires.* The mixed, often lamentable, consequences of violent revolution and reactionary measures to it are spelled out in *Battle of Algiers, Burn!, State of Siege, Ramparts of Clay, Khartoum,* and *Zulu.* Entertainment films and documentaries such as *The*

From Lindsay Anderson's If . . .

Borinage, The Bowery, and *Harlan County, USA* prick our consciences.

Therefore, when passed through the critical sieve of an informed social consciousness, motion pictures (and TV programs) can serve the goals of both humanism and liberation. And today the poor and the disenfranchised own TV and radio receivers; they have access to movies and pictorial journalism. If they do not find programs that directly serve their needs and aspirations for social ascent, they at least may begin to discern the strategy for recognizing their situation as well as the leaders, goals, tactics, and spectrum of consequences that participation and self-determination demand.

Movies can help redefine situations and shatter the mind-binding assumptions that tacitly are contained in the reality principle. The imagination is a revolutionary faculty: It presents alternatives. Lindsay Anderson's *If...* is an example of schoolboys in revolt. The final scene imagines a massacre of faculty, administrators, and parents—brutal but understandable in the light of the draconian system of education, so insensitive and repressive.

If... shows how bloody revolution is the inevitable consequence when the liberating process of humanization is systematically neglected. In short, as John F. Kennedy once observed, those who prevent peaceful revolution make bloody revolution inevitable. Motion pictures confirm this lesson. Film is a liberating force when taken as a global image of the deepest aspirations of the species and not only as an entertainment medium to divert and distract. This "reel" revolution is, to my way of thinking, the "revolutionary revolution."

INDEX

Photo Credits